**SCHOLASTIC**

# create and display

## Reading

**Full of exciting activities and displays for the whole curriculum**

**Ages 5–11**
for all primary years

**Liz Webster and Sue Reed**

Book End, Range Road, Witney, Oxfordshire, OX29 OYD
www.scholastic.co.uk

© 2010, Scholastic Ltd

1 2 3 4 5 6 7 8 9   0 1 2 3 4 5 6 7 8 9

British Library Cataloguing-in-Publication Data
A catalogue record for this book is available from the
British Library.

ISBN 978-1407-11915-1
Printed by Bell & Bain Ltd, Glasgow

Text © 2010 Scholastic Education on behalf of the
authors

Liz Webster and Sue Reed hereby assert their moral
rights to be identified as the authors of this work in
accordance with the Copyright, Designs and Patents
Act 1988.

**Commissioning Editor**
Paul Naish

**Editor**
Janice Baiton

**Series Designer and Cover Design**
Andrea Lewis

**Photography:**
Steve Forest

**Acknowledgements**
Liz Webster, Headteacher of Aldingbourne Primary
School, and Sue Reed, Deputy Headteacher,
would like to thank all the children and staff of
their school for their enthusiasm, hard work and
cooperation in the making of this book. They
would like to especially thank Wendy and Nicholas
Davies for their hard work and dedication and
amazing artwork! They would also like to thank
Steve Forest, the photographer, for always being
so helpful and easy to work with and incredibly
flexible. The authors and publishers would like to
say a big thanks to everybody who helped make
this book possible.

The following are registered trademarks:
King Arthur (Ravensburger AG; King Arthur
Industries Co Ltd; CA Foods Ltd; Obshchestvo s
ogranitchennoi otvetstvennostyou 'Intel'; James J.
Mitton)

Alice in Wonderland (Disney)

Winnie the Pooh (Disney)

Humpty Dumpty (Intex Syndicate Ltd; Société des
Produits Nestlé SA)

Hickory Dickory Dock (Littlewoods Ltd)

Robin Hood (Tiger Aspect Productions Ltd; Robin
Hood Telecom GmbH; Greatman International
Developments Ltd)

# Contents

In 'The Lion and The Mouse' I am kind when I help the lion.

Punctuation gives the reader clues to help them read the story.

# Introduction

- Welcome to *Create & Display: Reading*. Over recent years, learning to read has been highlighted as the most important skill that children can acquire as it provides a gateway for their learning. Once children can read, they have access to the 'world of words', and the more they read, the more new vocabulary they encounter. As their vocabulary grows, it improves their speaking skills and their writing. Reading introduces children to new ideas and concepts, which helps develop their understanding. Reading becomes a fundamental tool through which children can learn more. This book aims to show how reading can be taught and displayed through a creative, dynamic and fun approach.

## What do We Mean by Reading?

- Learning to read encompasses many skills. Children need to learn not only to apply a range of reading strategies to decode words with accuracy and some fluency but also to read with understanding and enjoyment.
- As children progress as readers, they will need to develop an interest and pleasure in reading, learn to read confidently and independently, read a range of materials, develop their own tastes and preferences and begin to reflect on the meaning of texts by analysing and discussing literature with others.

*Rhyming words are words that have the same sound at the end.*

## Practical Activities

- To learn to read, children need to be taught how to use a range of strategies to tackle unfamiliar words:
- **Phonic skills** can help to identify and blend phonemes (letter sounds) together to read words and explore sound patterns such as rhyme and alliteration.
- **Word recognition skills** can help them read on sight high-frequency words and other familiar words or parts of words.

- **Grammatical awareness** can help to predict unfamiliar words by re-reading or reading ahead and thinking about what might make sense.
- **Contextual understanding** can draw on their background knowledge and understanding of the content to help them to tackle tricky words.

## Understanding Texts

- It is vital that, alongside learning to read the words, children learn to read for meaning and make sense of what they read. They should learn to reflect on the meaning of texts, explore alternative meanings through

discussions with others and begin to develop ideas about which texts appeal to them and why, or why not. To develop their understanding of fiction, children should have the opportunity to explore and discuss characters and settings, events and plot lines, story language, patterns of rhythm and rhyme, and their own tastes and preferences. They should also have plenty of opportunity to respond imaginatively in different ways to stories and poems they have read.

## Investigating Types of Text

- It is important that children explore a range of text types, authors and genres. Breadth of study will enable children to learn about the characteristics of different types of text and to develop their own tastes and preferences. The range should include: stories and poems with familiar settings; stories and poems based on imaginary or fantasy worlds; adventure and mystery stories; myths, legends and fables; stories by significant children's authors; folk and fairy stories; stories and poems from a range of cultures; stories and poems with patterned or predictable language.

## Cross-curricular Links

- Throughout this book we have demonstrated that the most effective reading lessons are practical and exciting for the children. Each chapter offers a range of stimulating and original ideas that we use in our classrooms. The lessons move from the very early stages of developing phonic knowledge and skills in word recognition to exploring and experimenting with different text types once the children are established as confident and independent readers. At each stage they should be engaged in lively lessons in which fun and exciting games reinforce their learning and help them to develop into keen readers.

- *Create & Display: Reading* aims to help the reader in every aspect of teaching reading, from creating a reading environment within your school to planning and teaching reading lessons and whole units of work. The chapter 'Creating a Reading Culture' contains a range of themes full of practical advice on how to raise the profile of reading in your school. The subsequent chapters tackle how to plan and teach different genres of books with each theme following the same basic structure by including a whole-class starter, practical activities, display ideas and cross-curricular links. The final chapter, 'Stories from Favourite Authors', covers how to plan and teach an extended book study, looking in-depth at a book over a period of time.

Each lesson contains the following features:

- **Whole-class starter:** this is the starting point for each lesson, and to engage and stimulate the children it must be exciting, meaningful and relevant. Teaching strategies include teacher in role, children working with a 'talk partner' to discuss ideas, shared reading, lively games and visual props such as an interactive whiteboard.

- **Practical activities:** this part of the lesson reinforces the learning that has taken place during the whole-class starter session and must be equally exciting. We have included many practical ideas for different kinds of games as well as ideas for how to record work in an imaginative way.

- **Display ideas:** displaying work on reading within the school environment, raises the profile of reading as a fun and friendly subject and also gives children opportunities for further reading and writing through interacting with the display.

- **Cross-curricular links:** byways in which links can be made between reading and other curriculum areas to help learning become more relevant and meaningful for young children have been highlighted.

- So remember – reading is a fun and rewarding part of the curriculum for both child and teacher, and if taught imaginatively and comprehensively, it can provide a gateway for all other aspects of learning. Happy reading!

*Liz Webster and Sue Reed*

# Creating a Book Corner

## What is a Book Corner?

- A specific area in a classroom where the children access different types of books.
- These books could include any school reading scheme in addition to story books, picture books, fiction, non-fiction, topic-related books and poetry books.
- A place where children can sit and read books individually, with a friend or in a small group.
- A stimulating place that celebrates books and encourages reading.

## Setting up a Book Corner

- First, your book corner needs a theme to promote the pleasures of reading and to draw attention to the allocated area. It could be based on a topic you are studying or celebrate a particular author or simply be designed to inspire children to read. For example, if your topic is 'The Body', your book corner could have a skeleton theme titled 'Bone Shaking Books' and a skeleton with a speech bubble saying 'Rattle your way through a good book', or you could create an underwater scene titled 'Dive into a good book'.
- Involving children in creating a stimulating book corner is very important. If you want to set up your book corner for the beginning of the new academic year, you could undertake any artwork needed for the book corner during a day or session when your new class come to meet you. If this is not possible, the work could be achieved at the beginning of the new year.
- Organising the books is paramount for ensuring that your book corner is an inviting place to be. First sort through your books so that only quality books remain; for example, throw away any that are worn or inappropriate. When organising books for younger children, ensure that all picture books are arranged in easily accessible and labelled book boxes and that fiction or non-fiction books relate to your topic and are displayed separately so that children know where to find them.
- Books for older children can be organised in boxes according to their genre; for example, fantasy books, adventure stories, sport stories, classic authors. This allows children to think about the kind of books they are choosing and ensures that books can be returned to the correct boxes with ease.
- When training children to select books and put them back in the correct place, an 'I'm not sure box' could be useful. The children place their finished books in this box if they are not sure where it belongs. Together the class put the books away.

## Using the Book Corner

● Include a 'Teacher's top tips' section in the book corner listing ten of the teacher's

favourite books. Show these books to the children before they are added to the book corner and explain why you think they are great books. The teacher may choose whether to read the blurb or a section of the book to the children, leaving it on a cliffhanger, or to read a much-loved book again and again so it becomes a class favourite. Modelling this excitement about books is crucial in encouraging the children to enjoy reading.

● Give each child a personal reading diary or log. For younger children this is a place where parents and teachers log the reading that the child does at home and at school.

As the children become more independent, they should be encouraged to respond to their reading in their reading diaries, writing about and drawing pictures of parts of the book they have enjoyed, favourite characters, etc. They should also be encouraged to make comments on their tastes in reading; for example, why they have enjoyed/not enjoyed certain books, their favourite genres and authors.

● Create a magical atmosphere in the book corner by reading a story in this area daily. Make storytimes exciting – use different types of books, props, puppets, story sacks, candlelight, music to enhance the telling of a story.

## Ideas for Book Corner Themes

● **Jump into a jungle of books** – paint animals, colour mixed leaves, create jungle scenes, hide book titles among leaves, give animals speech bubble questions about books, such as 'What is your favourite book?'

● **Snap up a good book** – paint or collage large crocodile heads. In between the teeth put exciting, fun, interesting words to describe books.

● **Pedal your way through a paperback** – paint or attach a bicycle to the wall. On the spokes put words relating to different genres.

● **Burrow into a good book** – paint a giant bookworm. Use book stands to place lots of books around the bookworm. Children could copy the front cover of favourite book to stick on the front of their reading diary.

● **Use an author or illustrator as a book corner theme** – for example: *Waddell's World* (Martin Waddell); *Quirky Quentin* (Quentin Blake); *Dahl's Delights* (Roald Dahl); *Magical McKee* (David McKee); The Ahlbergs (Allan and Janet Ahlberg); *The Wonder of Wilson* (Jacqueline Wilson); *Foreman's Favourites* (Michael Foreman).

# Creating a Library

books. Computer software provides an exciting way to make your library child friendly and magical, just like a real library! For example, children can either have their own library card or number to enable them to loan a book.

- Create a timetable for use of the library and employ some older children as school librarians – a great honour!

## Setting up an Effective Library Environment

- Choose an appropriate place in the school to create a library. Ideally in a highly visible area, accessible to the children. However, if the only option is for your library to be 'tucked away', then signage is paramount!
- Purchase appropriate shelving and storage – make it child friendly.
- Audit existing stock. The quality of books is vital, so be ruthless with anything worn, old or uninviting.
- Purchase new stock. Introduce the idea of a 'sponsor a book' sale. Invite a local bookshop or Scholastic book club to attend the school with a selection of high-quality books. The children purchase the book and donate it to the school library. In the front of the book, make a label that reads 'This book was donated by ...'.
- Plan how to organise your books. Non-fiction needs to be classified and arranged by the Dewey system. Fiction can be organised in alphabetical order or in themes. Make labels that clearly show where children can find appropriate books.
- Devise a system for loaning and returning

## Opening and Promoting the Library

- Invite 'Mr Read' (teacher in role) to attend the school library opening. Introduce him as the person who has had a library card for the longest period of time. Explain that this means he is very old and wise. Mr Read enters and explains what a library is and how to be a good library member. Teacher in role must ensure that Mr Read is quite a comical and forgetful character. The aim of his visit is to establish library rules.
- Following the session with Mr Read, adopt the theme of 'Love our Library'. Using the poem 'Roses are red, Violets are blue, Sugar is sweet and so are you', ask the children to create poems about the library. For example, 'Roses are red, violets are blue, Open at lunchtimes, Just for you!'
- Take groups of children into the library for a 'tour' on the opening day. Show them how to find books, some 'highlights' of the stock, and how to borrow books and return them.
- Promote the library by giving children a 'reading journey' to complete. This should be a picture that includes ten steps, such as a frog with ten lily pads. Every time the children

visit the library, they collect a sticker for their reading journey. When they have completed their reading journey, they should be presented with a certificate in assembly and become a library VIP, which could mean that they get a special library card to take two books out at a time.

## Practical Activities within the Library

- Library Hunt. Create a treasure hunt based around learning to locate books in the library. Give the children a list of books to find. Show them how to use the computer software, code-breaker or Dewey system to locate the books. Inside each book a letter should be hidden. The children must write the letters down and unscramble them to spell a word or phrase about the library. If they are correct, they win a prize.
- Play 'Library Locations'. Split the group into two teams. Show the name of a book or author to a player from each team and they must race to find it as quickly as possible. The winner earns a point for their team.
- Design a poster advertising the library. Include slogans that advertise all the different features of the library.
- Play 'Mr Read's Racetrack'. Teacher should continue in role as Mr Read and work with a small group in the library. Make a giant racetrack playing board with a start and finish. Give each child a counter. The object of the game is to be the first to reach the finish line. Each child takes it in turn to pull a question or challenge out of a box. They must read the question and find the relevant book within a time limit. For example, 'Find me a picture of an Emperor penguin' – the child should find the book on penguins and look for a picture of an Emperor. Next to the

picture will be an instruction, such as 'Move forward 5 spaces'. If the children cannot complete the challenge in the given time, they cannot move.
- Prepare a set of cards with a series of numbers from the Dewey system written on it. The children must find that number and write down the subject of that section.

## Display Ideas

- The library needs a big 'Welcome to the Library' sign with keywords related to the library.
- Display instructions for borrowing and returning books.
- Display 'Love your Library' poems on love-heart shapes reinforcing library rules.
- Display photographs of librarians and library timetable.
- Display pictures of reading activities across the school; for example, reading independently, using the library, book buddies, group reading.
- Display children's posters advertising the library.

# Sight Vocabulary

## Common Words

- Children will begin to read by using their phonic knowledge to break down words. However, there are many words, including some of the most common ones, such as 'I' or 'was', for which this is not a helpful strategy, and so it is vital that children develop the skills to recognise these words by sight as early as possible. Teachers should explicitly teach such words to the whole class on a regular basis, beginning with the simplest common words. Teaching should include whole-class activities, small focused group activities and using the classroom environment.

## Whole-class Activities

- Introduce the class to a large, red, spiky laminated word. Explain that it is red because red means danger! This is a word they have to be careful of because it is a tricky word to spell. For example, if looking at the word 'was', discuss that it sounds as if it should be spelt 'w-o-s' but actually the 'a' in the middle is the tricky bit of the word because it sounds like an 'o'. Once a red word has been introduced to the children, it should be placed somewhere visible, such as on the ceiling, where the children can refer to it for spelling.

- Make a selection of games to play using an interactive whiteboard. These should include a range of 'red' words that you have taught to the children. Ideas could include (a) Rub and Reveal – words are hidden that can be revealed by rubbing away with an eraser. The children must guess which word it is as you rub and reveal it. (b) Countdown – prepare a selection of anagrams on the interactive whiteboard. Display one at a time and give the children a whiteboard and a pen. Play a timed piece of music and challenge the children to work out the word before the music ends. (c) Hangman – play hangman with one of the red words you have taught. (d) Prepare a giant wordsearch and challenge the children to find red words within it. (e) Use a spotlight tool to find red words and read them. (f) Prepare a multimedia presentation in which words flash in and out of sight quickly on the board – children must say them as they appear, getting quicker and quicker.

- Play 'Knock Down'. Split the class into groups of six to eight. Ask a group to stand up. Use the flash cards of the red words you have taught. Hold one up and ask the children to read it and shout it out. The person who reads it first is able to choose someone in the group to 'knock down' and that child is out of the game. The last child standing in each group is the winner and is entered into the final.

- Play 'Bin it or Bagsy it'. Split the class into two teams. Place a selection of words on the board. Some words must be spelt incorrectly. A member of each team takes it in turn to race to the board and pick a word. They must decide whether to bin the word because it is incorrect or bagsy it because it is correct.

## Group Activities

- Prepare a selection of laminated word finders that consist of the red words the children have been learning. Give each child a word finder, whiteboard and pen. Call out a word and roll a dice. The children must find the word and write it on their whiteboard the number of times shown on the dice.

- Play 'Grapes'. Prepare an enormous set of grapes on the board. On each grape write a word. Split the group into two teams and give each team a fly swatter. A member from each team stands in a hoop with their back to the board. The teacher calls out a word that is on one of the grapes. The children must quickly turn around and identify the correct word by swatting it with their fly swatter. The first child to identify the word correctly wins a point.
- Play 'Stepping Stones'. Prepare a selection of large stepping stones with a red word on

each. Place the stepping stones across the hall or carpet area. The children must attempt to cross the designated area using only the stepping stones. In order to step on a stone, they must be able to read its word correctly.

- Play 'Twister'. Use the well-known game Twister or make your own spotted coloured mat. Stick red words on each spot. The children take it in turn to spin the spinner and carry out the necessary instructions.
- Play 'Ready to Read'. Make a selection of shaped boards that contain some of keywords. Make a set of small cards that correspond with these words and pop them in a bag. The children take turns to pick a word and if they can read it and it is on their board, they are allowed to cover that word. The object of the game is to read and cover all the words on their board.

## Using the Classroom Environment

- Place all the red words that the children have learned on the ceiling. Refer to these words regularly. For example, at register time ask the children to read a word from the ceiling.
- Where appropriate, make mnemonics of keywords and display around the classroom. For example, because = Big Elephants Can Always Upset Small Elephants.

- Make giant pencils with keywords on and hang from the ceiling all around the classroom.
- Create a word wall, adding words as weeks go by.
- Make keyword mats or word finders for children to use on their tables as they are writing.

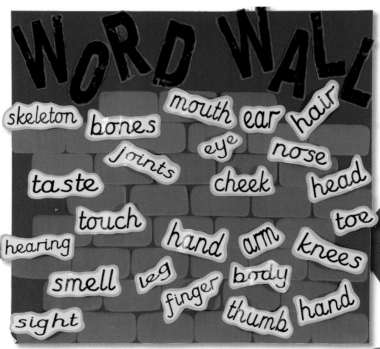

# Celebrating a Book Week

## Creating a Book Event

● A great way to promote the pleasures of reading is to come together as a school or a class for a book event. Here we provide a few examples that you may use or adapt to fit with your own theme or focus.

## Our Favourite Books

● In assembly the week prior to book week, ask the teachers to bring in their favourite children's book. Play 'Guess Who' in assembly. Can the children match the books to the teachers? Explain that next week's theme for Book Week is favourite books and that they must bring their favourite book to school on Monday.
● Plan a selection of activities for each class for the following week based around their favourite books, such as:
● Draw the front cover of their favourite book. Sort the class's favourite books into genres to find out what type of books are the most popular in your class.
● Write a sequel to their favourite story.
● Draw a character map for their favourite book

identifying the relationships between the characters.
● 'Read on the Ring' – children keep their favourite books with them at all times and every time the bell rings the whole class (including the teacher) should stop and read for 5 minutes.
● Spend a whole day planning and making a story sack to accompany their favourite book. Begin the day by looking first-hand at a range of story sacks plus the things they might include, such as props, puppets, games, quizzes, non-fiction books. The children should then plan their story sack on a design sheet and spend the day making the sack and its contents.
● Hold a favourite book fun day. Ask the children to come to school dressed up as a character from their favourite book and plan a day in which each class is involved in fun-filled activities related to favourite books.

## Comic Strips

● In the opening assembly at the beginning of book week, introduce the children to the genre of comic strips. Identify the features

of a comic strip and explain the history of the comic strip as a genre.

- Create a quiz that will test the children's knowledge of comic strips. On laminated book shapes, spell out the word 'comic strip' and on the back of each letter put a number that represents points to be won. Prepare a set of questions related to comic strips and place in a bag or box. Each team takes it in turn to pick a question. If they answer correctly, they choose a letter from the words *comic strip* and turn it over to reveal how many points they have won for their team.

- Collect a range of comic or annuals so that the children may have first-hand experience of comic strips.

- Compare old comics to new comics and look at the similarities and differences.

- Invite the children to plan and draw their own comic strip using familiar characters.

- Practise using speech and thought bubbles. Laminate some large comic strip pictures and ask the children to add their own speech and thought bubbles to the pictures.

- On a particular day in Book Week, invite the children to dress up as their favourite comic strip character. During the day the children could take part in activities relating to comics. This day could begin with a 'crazy' assembly in which a teacher in role as 'Walter the Softie' attempts to lead a sensible assembly based around comic strips when he is interrupted by another teacher in role as 'Dennis the Menace' who comes in and creates havoc!

## Fairy Tales

- In the opening assembly at the beginning of Book Week, introduce the children to the theme of fairy tales and explain that during this week each class will study a different fairy

tale. To begin the week, gather a selection of objects from different fairy tales and ask the children if they can match the objects to the correct fairy tale.

- Gather together a selection of different versions of the same fairy tale for each class or year group. These should include traditional, humorous, nonsense, etc.

- Focus on the traditional version of your fairy tale first. Discuss plot, characters, etc.

- Ask the children to write riddles or haiku poems relating to different fairy tales.

- Give the children a choice of how to represent the story, such as story map, zigzag book, cartoon strip, poem.

- Ask the children to write a fairy tale from a different character's point of view.

- Ask the children to write a modern version of a fairy tale.

- Hold a whole-school fairy tale fun day to finish off Book Week. The children should spend the day taking part in lots of activities relating to fairy tales. For example:

  - **Food technology** – bake gingerbread men.
  - **Drama** – put the children into groups of five, and according to the characters they are dressed up as, they invent a new fairy tale to perform.
  - **Music** – using the song 'There was a Princess Long Ago', invite the children to compose their own version based around a fairy tale of their choice.
  - **Outdoor Adventure Activity** – hide objects related to fairy tales as clues around the school. With each clue hide a letter. The children must collect all the letters and unscramble them to make words, such as *fairy tale*, *Cinderella*.
  - **D&T** – provide a range of construction kits and materials for the children to use. Make a set of challenge cards for the children, such as make a castle for the giant, make a broomstick for the witch, make a carriage for Cinderella.

# Respond to Your Reading

## Reading Diaries

- Most schools will use a reading diary or log where children and parents can note down books they have read. As children enter this independent phase, their reading diary or log should become a place where they are encouraged to respond to their reading. They should continue to note books they have read but also make comments about their reading. It is important at this stage to make it explicit to children that they are allowed to return books they are not enjoying but that they should reflect on what it was about the book they didn't like. This is a vital part of their development as they begin to make reading choices and develop their own preferences and tastes.

- Once children have completed a book, they should be asked to make a response in their reading diary. They could be given a list of activities to stick into their reading diary. Explain that they can choose any activity but should choose different ways to respond as far as possible. They should make sure they tick off an activity when they have completed it. Place a box in the classroom where children can leave their reading diary to be marked when they have completed an activity.

## Text Activities

- Write an alternative ending for the story.
- Re-write the story for a younger child.
- Take on the role one of the characters and talk about an event that has happened.
- With a partner, compose a freeze frame of a moment in the story. Take a photograph and write a caption for it.
- Choose a character from the story and write their diary.
- Describe characters' feelings at particular moments in the story.
- Use thought bubbles to show the differences between two characters.
- Put the characters into a different setting. How would they behave?
- Introduce a new character into the story – how would the others behave towards them?
- Produce a cartoon strip of the story.
- Summarise the plot.
- Write a list of the three most important moments in the story.
- List the key characters, events or features of the text.
- Retell an important event from the story.
- Retell the story in their own words.
- Write a review of the book.
- Create a character map following the characters' emotions and actions throughout the book.
- Draw a grid with two columns – in one column write what they definitely know about a character and in the other column write what they can guess about a character.
- Choose an event from the story. Why do the characters behave in the way that they do? What would they have done in the situation?
- Compare and contrast two settings in the story.
- Compare and contrast two characters in the story.
- Read the description of the setting and then draw it.

- Draw a map of the setting.
- Draw one of the characters and label with quotations from the text.

## Word/Sentence Activities

- Replace all the adjectives on one page, keeping the meaning the same.
- Find and memorise a phrase or a sentence to steal for their own writing. Copy it into their book three times to help remember it.
- List exciting adjectives from the text.

- List exciting verbs from the text.
- Find examples of adverbs.
- Find examples of complex sentences.
- Find short sentences that build suspense.
- Choose a sentence and then re-order the words keeping the meaning the same.

## Research Activities

- Research facts that link to the theme of the book.
- Find other books that have similar plots, themes or characters.
- Find out facts about the author or illustrator of the book.
- Find other books written by the author and list them.

... using thought bubbles to show the differences between two characters.

by ...

... writing a book review.

# Each Peach Pear Plum

## Whole-class Starter

- Read and enjoy the book *Each Peach Pear Plum* by Janet and Allan Ahlberg (Puffin Books). Discuss with the children what type of book it is. Explain that the book rhymes and this helps us when we are reading the story. Re-read the book but this time leave out the rhyming words and ask the children to supply these. For example, you read 'Cinderella down the stairs, I spy ...' and the children say 'Three Bears'.
- Play 'Ring the Rhyme'. Create a multimedia presentation that teaches about rhyme. Show the children a large picture in the middle of the interactive whiteboard. Around this picture put a selection of smaller pictures, one of which should rhyme with the large picture. Invite a child to circle the picture that rhymes. Extend this activity to words. Discuss what the children notice about words that rhyme. Look at the spelling patterns related to the rhyming

## Focus of Learning
**To use rhyming patterns as cues for reading**

words. Finally extend this to a sentence. Put a sentence on the board and ask the children to read it and complete the rhyme. For example, 'Tom Thumb on a boat, I spy a billy ... '. Include sentences where the rhyming words have different spelling patterns. For example, 'Tom Thumb asleep at night, I spy Snow ... '. Discuss this with the children.
- Play 'Run to the Rhyme'. In a large space or hall, place a selection of large pictures of fairytale or nursery rhyme characters. Give each child a card with a picture and a word that rhymes with one of the characters. On a given signal, the children must run to the appropriate character. For example, 'Three Bears' could be a large picture and the

children could be given a card with a picture of stairs or bears on it. Discuss the children's decisions and together look at the spellings.

- Play 'Round up your Rhymes' using the cards from the previous game. Give each child a card. Ask them to walk around the room whispering their rhyming word. When they hear somebody with a word that rhymes, they round them up until they have a complete rhyming gang.

## Practical Activities

- Play 'I Spy a Rhyme'. Make a set of large magnifying glasses that have rhyming clues relating to part of the school and a fairy tale character that the children will find there, but omit the character's details. For example, 'A place where teachers drink their tea, I spy the Princess and the... '. The children should go to the staffroom and find the next clue.
- Ask the children to write their own *Each Peach Pear Plum* rhymes. For example, 'Cinderella at the ball, I spy Humpty sat on the Wall. Goldilocks breaks the chair, I spy Rapunzel's golden hair'.
- Play 'Rhyming Dominoes'. Make a set of cards that have a rhyming word at each end. Deal out the dominoes to the players. Each player takes it in turns to lay a card. Players can lay a card if one of their cards rhymes with a card that has already been placed down on the table. The object is to get rid of all your cards.
- Play 'Rhyming Riddles'. Make a set of riddle cards based on the book *Each Peach Pear Plum*. On each riddle the final rhyming word should be missing. Using the interactive whiteboard, make a large bunch of plums that have the missing rhyming words on them. Split the class into two teams. Choose a

*Rhyming words are words that have the same sound at the end.*

player from each team. On a signal, give them a riddle to read. Each player must read the riddle, look for the correct rhyming word and place their card on the correct rhyming plum. The first player to do it gets points or a treat.

## Display Ideas

- Draw and watercolour large characters from the story.
- Colour mix, pastel and paint large plums, peaches and pears.
- Ask the children to draw and colour their own picture with hidden characters from the story.

## Cross-curricular Links

- **ICT** – Use an ICT photo package. Ask the children to edit photographs of themselves to look like a fairy tale or nursery rhyme character.
- **Literacy** – Read alternative versions of fairy tales and discuss the differences.
- **Maths** – Investigate how many fairy tales or nursery rhymes the children know. Investigate their favourites and represent the results in different ways, such as pie charts.

# Humpty Dumpty

## Whole-class Starter

- Read a variety of nursery rhymes. Encourage the children to join in with the ones they know. Discuss that these are well-known poems called nursery rhymes. Explain that they are called nursery rhymes because they used to be taught to the children in the nursery. Explain what the term 'rhyme' means. For example, words that have the same sound at the end.

- Play 'Guess the Nursery Rhyme'. Read parts of nursery rhymes and ask the children to complete the rhyme or fill in any missing words. For example, 'Hickory dickory ... or 'Baa Baa Black sheep have you any ...

- Read the rhyme 'Humpty Dumpty'. Discuss what the rhyme means. Ask the children to identify the words that rhyme and then to think of other words that rhyme with these words. For example, *wall* rhymes with *call*, *ball*, *stall*, *hall*, etc.

- Play 'Splat the Rhyme'. Prepare a selection of words on an interactive whiteboard or a

## Focus of Learning

To read and enjoy a number of nursery rhymes
To begin to understand what a nursery rhyme is

wall. Prepare another set of words on cards that rhyme with the words on the wall. Two children stand with their backs to the board or wall. Give each child a fly swatter. Call out a word and the children quickly turn around and splat the word that they think rhymes with that word.

- Play 'Egg Factor'. Make a set of laminated eggs that have been cracked in half. Each half should have one word from a pair of rhyming words on it. Make one half of the egg blue and the other half yellow. For example, on the blue half could be the word *wall* and on the yellow half the word *ball*. Give each child a piece of broken egg. On a given signal, the children move around the classroom and find their rhyming partner. Explain that if they have a blue piece of egg, they must find a yellow piece. Repeat several times.

## Practical Activities

- Give the children a nursery rhyme and ask them to act it out through mime. The children can then perform the rhyme to the other children in the group. Can they guess the rhyme?
- Play 'Crack an Egg'. Make a set of eggs with words on them. Place the eggs on the floor in a large space or outside area. Organise the children into two teams. Give each team a bouncer. The teacher calls out a word or shows the children a word. The children must read the word and then bounce as quickly as they can to the corresponding rhyming word. The first child to bounce on the correct egg wins a point for their team.
- Play 'Humpty Dumpty'. Make a set of tin cans with Humpty Dumpty on the front. (you will need lots of cans). Inside each can place a rhyming word. Place the cans on a brick wall or one made from large ploastic bricks. the children take it in turns to throw a ball at the cans. they must attempts to knock down two Humpty dumptys. If the words in the cans rhyme, the children collect a piece of Lego® and put it on their Lego® board. The object is to build the highest wall.

- Play 'The King's Men'. Make a set of Humpty Dumpty cards that are cut in half. On each half write part of a keyword. For example, *today* – one half would have *to* written on it and the other *day*. Place all the cards in the middle of a table. Give each child a crown to wear to represent the king's men. The children take it in turns to pick two Humpty Dumpty cards, a top and a bottom. If the words make a keyword, they keep the completed Humpty

Dumpty. The object is to collect as many completed eggs as possible.

## Display Ideas

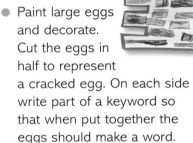

- Paint and collage a large Humpty Dumpty for display.
- Colour mix a selection of bricks for display. Ask the children to create different shades of red.
- Paint large eggs and decorate. Cut the eggs in half to represent a cracked egg. On each side write part of a keyword so that when put together the eggs should make a word.

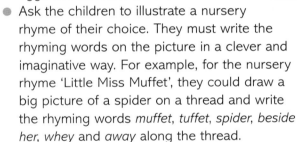

- Ask the children to illustrate a nursery rhyme of their choice. They must write the rhyming words on the picture in a clever and imaginative way. For example, for the nursery rhyme 'Little Miss Muffet', they could draw a big picture of a spider on a thread and write the rhyming words *muffet*, *tuffet*, *spider*, *beside her*, *whey* and *away* along the thread.
- Ask the children to paint their own version of Humpty Dumpy.

## Cross-curricular Links

- **Literacy** – Read the story *Little Lumpty* by Miko Imai (Walker Books). Discuss what Little Lumpty had done wrong in the story. Ask the children to write a letter to Little Lumpty expressing their horror that he disobeyed his mother.
- **Outdoor Adventure Activity** – Invite the children to work in teams to design and make an egg carrier that will protect Humpty Dumpty if he falls off the wall. Give them a selection of materials and organise a test to evaluate their product.
- **Art** – Give each child a hard-boiled egg and challenge them to turn the egg into a character of their choice, such as a pirate egg, a princess egg, a doggy egg.

# Hickory Dickory Dock

## Whole-class Starter

● Read and enjoy the nursery rhyme 'Hickory Dickory Dock'. Add actions to the song to help the children remember the words. Play 'Head Shoulders Knees and Toes' but using the nursery rhyme 'Hickory Dickory Dock'. The children say the rhyme using actions once all the way through. Next time they miss a line but still perform the action. This continues until children are only performing actions.

● Show the children a huge version of 'Hickory Dickory Dock' on the interactive whiteboard. Remove some of the words. Read the rhyme with the children and ask them to suggest what the missing words could be. Explain that because they know the

## Focus of Learning
**To learn to use a variety of reading strategies to tackle unfamiliar words**

rhyme by heart, it helps them to guess words when they are reading. Show them another familiar nursery rhyme, such as 'Jack and Jill', and see if they can read the words. Discuss how there are a range of strategies we can use to help us read unfamiliar words, such as using rhyme, letter sounds, picture clues and words that make sense.

● In pairs, give the children the second verse of 'Jack and Jill', which is not so familiar, and a lolly stick. They take it in turns to attempt to read the poem using the lolly stick as a pointer. Show a large version on the interactive whiteboard and discuss the words the children found tricky and the strategies they used.

- Ask the children to work in groups of three or four. Tell them they are going to write a new version of 'Hickory Dickory Dock' with the clock striking a different time. Explain that they must think about the rhyme and whether it makes sense or not. They must also create actions to match their rhyme. For example:

  *The clock struck four,*
  *There was a knock at the door.*
  *Hickory Dickory Dock,*
  *Knock, knock.*

## Practical Activities

- Children write and illustrate their version of 'Hickory Dickory Dock'. They could be encouraged to change the line 'Hickory Dickory Dock'.
  For example:
  *Hickory Dickory Dong,*
  *The mouse sang a song.*
  *The clock struck three,*
  *The mouse said 'Hee! Hee!'*

- Play 'Read and Rhyme'. Make a selection of large laminated nursery rhymes with six words missing from each rhyme. Put the missing words on separate cards in a bag or box on the table. The children take turns to pick a word out. If the word corresponds to their nursery rhyme, they place it in the correct place. If it does not, they put it back and miss a go. The object is to complete their nursery rhyme.

- Play 'Pelmanism Pairs'. Make two sets of cards, one with pictures from nursery rhymes, such as a clock, hill, spider, garden, wall, egg, kettle, the other with corresponding words. Place the cards face down on the table. The children take it in turns to pick two cards and if they match the picture with the corresponding word, they may keep their cards. If not, they must put them back and the next child has a turn. Discuss different strategies for tackling the words.

- In a small group, give the children a selection of nursery rhymes to read together. Read them and discuss the different strategies they have used to tackle the trickiest words. An additional extension to this game is to play 'Traffic Lights'. Give each child a red, green and yellow pen or pencil. Ask them to mark three words in green that they found easy to read, three in yellow that they had to stop and think about and three in red that they found very challenging. Discuss the children's choices with them.

## Display Ideas

- Paint and collage a large grandfather clock and mouse for display.
- Invite the children to draw and paint their own clocks.
- On the display produce a large version of Hickory Dickory clock. Omit words and replace with question marks. This will encourage the children to read the rhyme and attempt to put in the correct words.

- Print and cut out cogs of different sizes to use for the boarder on the display.

## Cross-curricular Links

- **D&T** – Using a pulley system, ask the children to produce a 3D clock and a mouse that can move up and down the clock.
- **Maths** – Focus on telling the time. Discuss *o'clock* on analogue and digital clocks.
- **Literacy** – Discuss the phoneme *ck*. How many other words can the children find that have *ck* in them?

# Jack and the Beanstalk

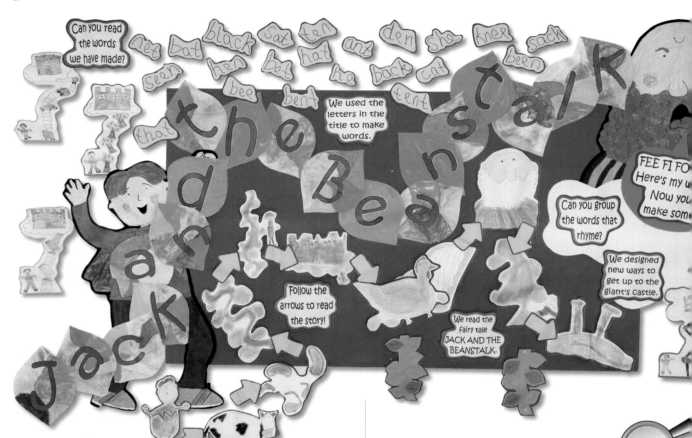

Can you read the words we have made?

We used the letters in the title to make words.

FEE FI FO
Here's my u
Now you
make som

Can you group the words that rhyme?

We designed new ways to get up to the giant's castle.

Follow the arrows to read the story!

We read the fairy tale JACK AND THE BEANSTALK.

## Whole-class Starter

- Read and enjoy the story *Jack and the Beanstalk*. There are several versions available by various authors. Ask the children questions about the story and discuss its events in detail.
- Introduce the children to the word *plot* and explain that this is the series of events that occur in the story. Show them a selection of pictures that relate to the story. Label each picture with a letter. Give each child a whiteboard and pen. Ask them which picture they think comes first in the story. The children must write the letter from the picture on their whiteboards. Discuss their answers. Continue until

We read the fairy tale JACK AND THE BEANSTALK.

## Focus of Learning
To read and enjoy the story of Jack and the Beanstalk
To sequence the events in the story

all the pictures have been organised into the correct order.
- Play 'Wordsearch'. Make a selection of words that relate to the sequence of the story; for example, *cow*, *beans*, *beanstalk*, *giant*, *hen* and *chop*. Give each child a word. On a given signal, they must walk around until they have found

a group that includes children with all six different words. Discuss the importance of each word and what they tell us about the story plot.

- Ask the children to look at the title of the story 'Jack and the Beanstalk'. Discuss with them the letters within the title. Model how you can make other words by using the letters from the title; for example, back, talk, ant, then. Give each child a laminated leaf and explain that they are going to make a giant word beanstalk. Ask each child to use the letters from the title to write a word. Invite each child to place their leaf on the board to make a beanstalk.

## Practical Activities

- Ask the children to draw their own story map, focusing on the main events of the story.
- Play 'Build a Beanstalk'. Make a large selection of laminated leaves and place in a basket. Make a dice that has leaves on four sides, a giant's face on one side and an axe on one side. The children take it in turns to roll the dice. If they roll a leaf, they must write a word on a laminated leaf using the letters from the title and place it on the wall or board.

The object is to collect as many leaves as possible and build a beanstalk. If they roll a giant, they must remove one of their leaves, and if they roll an axe, they must remove all their leaves. The child who has built the tallest beanstalk at the end of the game is the winner.

- In small groups, ask the children to retell the story in their own words. Record the children and use the CDs in the listening corner.

## Display Ideas

- Collage and paint a large Jack and a large giant for display.
- Divide giant leaves into segments and on each part use a different medium, such as oil pastels, felt tips, crayons, chalk pastels.
- Ask the children to think creatively about the end of the story. The beanstalk has been cut down, so how might Jack get to the giant's castle now? For example, he might stack fire engines on top of each other and climb up the ladders. Ask the children to draw their ideas and add colour using colouring pencils.
- Invite the children to draw giant pictures of the main events from the story. They could work in groups of ten and each child could decide on a different part of the story to draw. Add colour using chalk pastels.

## Cross-curricular Links

- **Science** – Grow your own beanstalk using runner beans or other seasonal plants.
- **Maths** – Give each child a laminated bean-stalk. Ask them to walk around the school and find things that are shorter, longer and the same length as their beanstalk.
- **Drama** – Ask the children to work in groups of six to act out the story. Give them a selection of props. An extension to this would be for them to write a play script for their play.

# The Three Billy Goats Gruff

## Focus of Learning
**To identify within a fairy tale the features of a good character and bad character**
**To discuss how these features are developed throughout the story**

## Whole-class Starter

- Read and enjoy the story *The Three Billy Goats Gruff* by Nick Sharatt and Stephen Tucker (Macmillan Children's Books). Show the children a list of fairy-tale features and discuss the features in the story that match the features of a fairy tale. For example, talking animals, the number three, strong moral, good versus bad.

- Introduce the children to the character of the troll. Ask them to discuss what a troll is and what makes the troll a bad character. Give each child a sticky note and ask them to write a word or phrase on it. Invite the children to stick their note on the interactive whiteboard. If possible, scan in a picture of the troll on the

board for the children to put their notes on. Discuss bad characters from other fairy tales. Make a mind map of bad characters.

- Play 'Baddie Bonanza'. Give each child a whiteboard and a pen. Prepare a selection of clues that relate to different bad characters in various fairy tales; for example, Big Bad Wolf, Captain Hook, Giant, Evil Stepmother, Ugly Sisters, Wicked Witch. The children must use the clues to help them identify the baddie. Ask them to write their

answer on a whiteboard. Reveal the answer via a picture on the interactive whiteboard.

- Show the children the word *troll* on the interactive whiteboard. Ask them to say, shout and whisper the word. Show the word *troll* but place sound buttons underneath each part of the word tr o ll.
- Ask the children what they think about this word. Explain that the final sound is tricky because even though it has two 'll's you only say one 'l'. Compose a simple piece of text for the children to use. Ensure that they can read the text. Working in pairs with a small pointer, ask them to try to recognise words in the text that have double letters. Discuss their answers and highlight the double letters in each word as you write them on the board.

## Practical Activities

- Give each child a description of a bad character from a fairy tale. Ensure that they can read the description. Ask them to read the text carefully and then draw the character using the description in the text to help them.
- Play 'Mix and Match'. Ask the children to work in groups of three and give each member a piece of A3 paper. Fold the paper into three parts.

In the top part the children must draw the head of a bad character. This should be done in secret so the other members do not see. The children pass their paper around to the next person and this time they draw the body of a baddie. Once again this must be done secretly. They pass the paper to the next person. Finally, at the bottom of the paper they draw the feet of a bad character. They then open up their paper to reveal a funny 'mix and match' bad character.

- Make a set of picture lotto boards and a set of cards showing words that have double letters in them. Place the cards in a bag or feely box. The children take it in turn to pick a word, read it and match it to the corresponding picture on their picture board. To make the game more exciting, if they pick out a card showing the word *troll*, they must remove all their cards from their board.

## Display Ideas

- Paint and collage a giant troll and the three billy goats. Colour mix a selection of shades of brown for bricks and use them to create a bridge across the display board.
- Ask the children to paint and collage their own mean and nasty troll.
- Ask the children to make a selection of puppets that represent the characters. Invite them to perform a play using their puppets.
- Make a clay troll.
- Ask the children to draw a character of their choice in a pose that represents a word that has a double letter, such as a billy goat kissing the troll. They should write the word *kiss* in *large bubble* writing.

## Cross-curricular Links

- **Literacy** – Invite the children to create a bad character and to write a fairy tale that includes their newly created 'baddie'.
  - **Maths** – Focus on counting in threes and the three times table.
  - **D&T** – Using a construction kit, ask the children to build a bridge to support a given weight.

# Traditional Tales from Other Cultures

## Whole-class Starter

- Explain that you are going to tell the children a traditional tale from Africa. A traditional tale is one that has been passed down through generations and was often told orally to children before bedtime. Create a campfire scene using logs and false flames. Invite the children to sit around the campfire in a darkened room. Retell an African tale in your own words, such as *How the Zebra got his Stripes* by Justine and Ron Fontes (Golden Books).
- Depending on the age and the ability of the children, either invite them to read a selection of African tales or use adults to read the

## Focus of Learning

**To enjoy reading a selection of African tales**

**To begin to understand the features of a traditional tale**

tales to small groups. After the children have listened or read a selection, discuss the features of a traditional African tale. Create a whole-class mind map to illustrate these features; for example, told orally, passed down through generations, includes animals, and teaches a moral lesson.
- Use the words *African Tale* and ask the children to write an acrostic poem

that explains what an African Tale is. For example:

**A** *tale from long ago*
**F** *or children*
**R** *eminds us of lessons to be learned*
**I** *ncludes a moral*
**C** *rowded around a fire a tale is told*
**A** *nimals are often in them*
**N** *ight-time story*
**T** *old over the years*
**A** *lternate versions of the same tale*
**L** *essons are learned*
**E** *verlasting stories*

## Practical Activities

- In small groups, ask the children to read a selection of tales and identify the features discussed in the carpet session. As a group, create a multimedia presentation to highlight what they have discovered.
- In small groups, ask the children to pick a traditional tale and practise telling the story orally. Encourage them to use instruments to enhance the story. Record the children retelling the tales. Place the recordings in the listening corner so others can enjoy the tales.
- In a feely box, place the names of lots different African animals. The children pick out two animals and work with a partner to create a new African tale.
- Provide a selection of props and masks that relate to several African tales. In small groups, ask the children to act out a tale of their choice. Encourage them to perform their play using mime. This will develop their acting and expressive skills.

## Display Ideas

- Pick an African tale that the children have enjoyed. Ask them to draw and chalk pastel the main features of the story. Use the pictures to create a story map. Ask the children to write speech bubbles that correspond with the pictures. Use these to create a display. Include labels that highlight the features of a traditional African tale.
- Invite the children to paint an African sunset using shades of red, orange and yellow. Use

black paint and a very thin paintbrush to create a silhouette scene.
- Ask the children to pick an African animal. Using wax crayons and focusing on the animal skin pattern, ask the children to camouflage their chosen animal into a similar pattern background.

- Create an African animal jigsaw. Give each child a picture of an African animal. Ask them to cut the picture into strips and re-stick the picture onto a blue background but leave gaps between each strip. This creates an 'exploding animal' type effect.

## Cross-curricular Links

- **Music** – Invite an African drummer to host a drumming workshop using a variety of African drums.
- **Geography** – Take the children on an imaginary magic carpet ride across Africa. Visit lots of African landmarks such as, pyramids, Victoria Falls, Sahara Desert, Kenya on safari. After they have returned from their amazing adventure, ask the children to draw the landmarks on a map of Africa.

- **D&T** – Using a range of construction kits, ask the children to build their own jungle scene and animals.

# What is Poetry?

## Whole-class Starter

- Read the children your favourite poem. Ask them if they know what you have just read and what it is called. Explain that today they are going to be learning about poetry. Ask if anybody can give you a definition of the word poetry. Discuss what a poem is with the children.

- Give each child a whiteboard and pen. In pairs, ask them to discuss the different types of poetry; for example, rhyming, non-rhyming, limerick, riddle. Together create a giant mind map of different types of poems.

- Give each pair a whiteboard and pen. Read a poem to the children. They must decide together what type of poem they think it is. They write their answer on the whiteboard and hold up the answer. Discuss their reasons for choice.

- Play 'Poetic Pairs'. Make two sets of envelopes. One set should contain a type of poem, and the other an example of that poem. Give each child an envelope and on a signal they open their envelopes and try to find their partner.

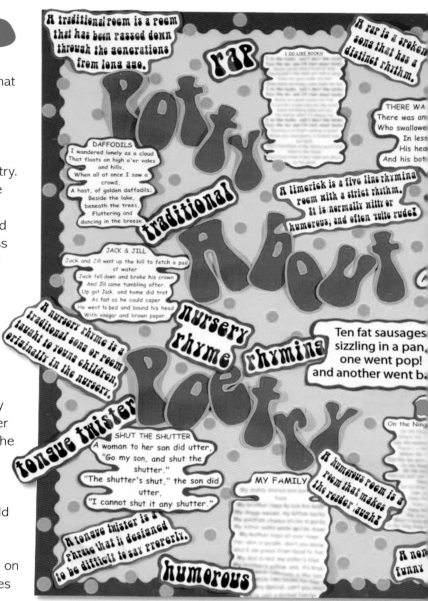

## Practical Activities

- Provide a selection of different types of poems. In small groups, ask the children to read, enjoy and discuss the poems. Do they notice any particular features? Which poems do they like or not like?

- Ask the children to choose a poem to perform to the class. Encourage them to use props and actions to enhance their performance. Each group could perform their poem at the end of the session.

### Focus of Learning
To understand what poetry is
To discuss the different types of poetry available to us
To begin to classify types of poems

- Play 'Puzzle over a Poem'. Make a selection of different types of poems and number them 1 to 20. Give each child a laminated sheet with a grid labelled 1 to 20. The children must read the poems and decide what type of poem they are reading. They must record this next to the appropriate number on their laminated sheet. For example, if poem number 4 is a riddle, they would write *riddle* next to the number 4 on their sheet. Make a class anthology of favourite poems. Set the children a piece of homework to find their favourite poem. Ask them to write and illustrate their work. Create an anthology of poems that can be shared at regular intervals with the class. This could be achieved by ringing a bell and saying it is 'pause for a poem' time.

## Display Ideas

- Create a chequered board with the title 'Potty about Poetry'. Make a collection of different types of poems that represent the different genres. Enlarge the poems and ask the children to illustrate them appropriately.
- Ask the children to write large labels for the display explaining the features of the different types of poems.
- Ask the children to choose their favourite poem and rewrite it using pictograms to replace keywords.

## Cross-curricular Links

- **Music** – Using a poem as a stimulus, ask the children to add sound effects to create a soundtrack for the poem.

> What am I?
> Lives in winter,
> Dies in summer,
> And grows with its root upwards.

root

- **History** –
  Look at classic poets and discuss the reasons why these poems are still famous today.
- **Literacy** – Ask the children to pick a poem and learn to recite it by heart.

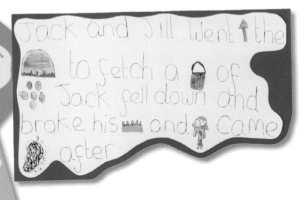

# Shape Poems

A shape poem....

...always has a shape.

...can be a collection of words.

...can be rhyming or non-rhyming.

...can take any form.

We have written our own shape poems.

A calligram is a one-word shape poem.

We ha writt our c calligr

## Whole-class Starter

- Divide the class into small groups and give them a selection of shape poems. Ask the children to read and discuss the poems. Gather the children together and ask them what they notice about the poems. Create a mind map of the different features of a shape poem. For example:
  - Always has a shape.
  - Can be rhyming and non-rhyming.
  - Can be a selection of words.
  - Can be simple sentences.
  - Can take any form.
  - Sounds good.
- Does not need to make sense.
- Show the children a shape poem that has no shape. Give each pair a whiteboard and ask them to design a shape to go with the poem.

## Focus of Learning
To understand the features of shape poems including calligrams

Select different children to show their shape poems.
- Introduce the children to a shape poem that is made up of one word. Explain that this type of shape poem is called a calligram. Prepare a selection of calligrams on

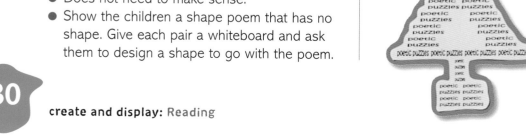

the interactive whiteboard. Ask what they notice.

- In pairs, give each child a whiteboard and pen. On the interactive whiteboard, show the children a word and ask them to write it as a calligram poem. Share ideas.

## Practical Activities

- Make a selection of words and place them in a bag or box. Children take turns to select a word and make it into a calligram poem. Ask them to write and illustrate the poem on large sheets of paper and use for display.
- Explain that they are going to write their own shape poem. As a group, choose a word and together make a shopping list of words that relate to that word; for example, *water = tap, drip, drop, river, stream, rain, sparkling, blue, wet, ripple, wave*, etc. The children can use these words to make a shape poem. For example, they may draw a tap and have the words in water droplets coming out of the tap. Discuss the different ways children have represented the words in their shape poems.
- Play 'Poetry Puzzles'. Make a selection of shape poems that are in a shape but replace the words from the poem with the words *poetic puzzles* over and over. Place the poems around the school or large space. The children must visit each poem, look at the shape and try to decide what the poem is about. On the back of the card will be the correct version of the poem. Once the children have guessed, they turn the poem over to see if they are correct.

- Give the children a selection of shape poems to read. Discuss the different features and why they think the author has represented the poem in that way. Can they think of other ways to represent the poem?

## Display Ideas

- Ask the children to choose an object and write a shape poem about it. Present the shape poem on a large piece of paper for display. Discuss grouping the words according to their subject. For example, if the poem was about a face, all words about 'hair' could be written in the shape of the hair.

It's great tobe a Castle,
With turrets tall and thin,
I can look down at the Jousting,
And see which knights going to win!

It's great to be a bubble,
Transparent and round,
I float up, up, up
And then down to the ground.
POP!

It's great to be an apple,
With skin shiny and red,
I hang from the tree until I am ripe,
And then I might fall on your head!

- As a whole class, create a shape poem for display. Pick a word or topic and ask each child to write a word or phrase about the topic. Together arrange the words to make a large shape poem on the display board.

## Cross-curricular Links

- **Maths** – Look at shapes in the environment. Learn about 2D and 3D shapes.
- **Literacy** – Vocabulary work. Ask the children to make a shopping list of words they might use in a shape poem. Classify the words according to nouns, verbs, adjectives etc.
- **Art** – Use the artist Giuseppe Arcimboldo (1527–93) as an example of an artist who uses pictures or real-life objects to represent shapes.

# Rhyming and Non-Rhyming Poems

## Whole-class Starter

- In role, enter the class as the knave from the rhyming kingdom all upset because you can write really good poems but they don't rhyme and the Queen of Rhyme keeps threatening to chop off your head. You have tried to explain that you do not understand what the difference is between a rhyming and non-rhyming poem but she will not listen. Ask the children if they could help. Read two poems, one that rhymes and one that does not. Ask the children to explain the differences. Encourage them to talk about the use of words that rhyme and the different rhythms within the poems.
- You are really excited that you now know the differences between the two. Explain that you have placed a selection of poems around the classroom or hall area. You would like the children to read the poems and decide if they rhyme or not. If they rhyme, the children must record two words that rhyme from that

### Focus of Learning
### To identify rhyming and non-rhyming poems

poem. Give them an A4 sheet to record their answers. Discuss their answers.

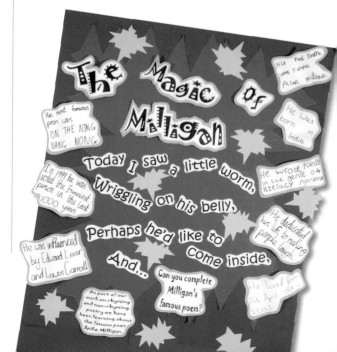

Teacher in role as a very angry Queen of Rhyme enters the classroom. She is cross because the knave has written a non-rhyming poem. But she is also cross with the children because they have encouraged this behaviour. They have taught him about non-rhyming and in her kingdom these are not good examples of poetry. She suggests that they only learn these types of poems because they are not clever enough to write rhyming poems. She explains that she is going to teach them how to write a rhyming poem. She uses the poem 'Today I Saw a Little Worm' by Spike Milligan (*Silly Verses for Kids*, Puffin Books) as a model and writes a new version.

For example:

*Today I saw a little pig,*
*Rolling in the mud,*
*Perhaps he'd like to build a house,*
*And eat a tasty spud.*

The Queen of Rhyme asks the children to work with a partner to write a rhyming poem using the same model. They share their poems with the queen.

## Practical Activities

- Ask the children to write and illustrate a rhyming poem using either the above poem as a model or a different rhyming poem as a framework; for example 'On the Ning Nang Nong' by Spike Milligan. Use the same poem structure but change the words. For example:

*On the ping pang pong,*
*Where the pigs go wrong,*
*And the monkeys all say YAHOO!*
*There's a pong pang ping,*
*Where the trees all sing,*
*And the mums go hibber habber hoo!*
*On the pong ping pang,*
*All the bees go bang,*
*And you just can't chase' em when they do!*

- Create a class anthology of favourite rhyming poems and favourite non-rhyming poems. Ask the children to look through a selection of poetry books and choose some rhyming and non-rhyming poems they like. Ask the children to copy their

poems and place them in the class anthology book.

- Play 'Race and Rhyme It!' Using the poem 'Today I Saw a Little Worm' by Spike Milligan as a model, rewrite a large selection of the poem using different words and rhymes. Miss out the initial rhyme or the final rhyme. Make

a selection of rhyming cards that correspond with the missing rhymes in the poem. In a large space or hall, divide your group into two teams and sit them on a mat or in a hoop. Place the individual words around the room. Read out the poem but miss out a rhyming word. The children discuss what the word could be, and at the sound of a hooter, one child from the group races to find the correct rhyming word. Discuss their choices.

- Make up a selection of poems that have some of their rhyming words missing. Ask the children to read the poems and attempt to put in the correct rhyming words. Discuss their decisions or choices.

## Display Ideas

- Paint and collage a large queen and knave for display.
- Ask the children to write up their rhyming poems and illustrate them for the display.
- Ask the children to write large captions of vocabulary associated with poetry; for example, rhyme, rhythm, rhyming couplets.

## Cross-curricular Links

- **Music** – Give the children a rhyming poem and ask them to create a sound using percussion instruments for each rhyming pair in the poem.
- **Literacy** – Learn about Spike Milligan the poet. Ask the children to research and write a biography about the key features in his life.
- **History** – Discuss with the children the punishment that often occurred in medieval times.

# Humorous Poems

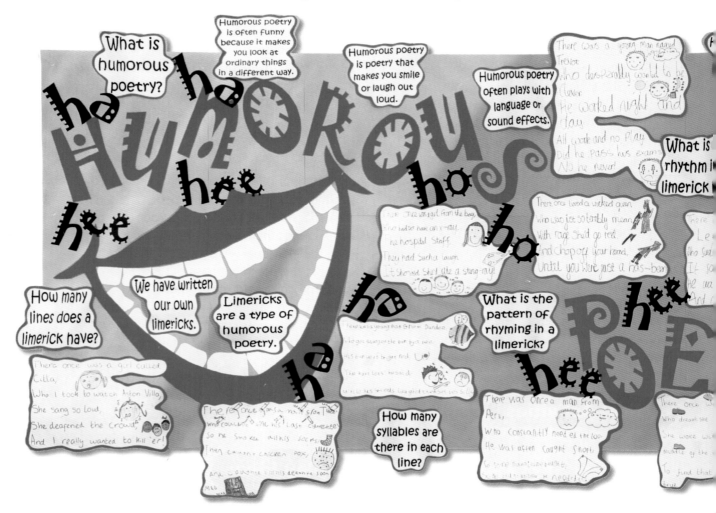

## Whole-class Starter

- Tell the children that they are going to focus on humorous poems. Ask them if they can give you an example of a type of humorous poem, such as limerick, riddle, nonsense, rhyming and non-rhyming poems. Explain that the main feature of a humorous poem is that it can come in any form but it must make you smile or laugh. Read and show the children a selection of different humorous poems.
- Present the children with an A3 laminated sheet of humorous poems. In pairs, ask them to decide on the type of poem and which poem they like best. Invite the children to rate the poems according to which ones they find the most humorous and explain their reasons.
- Explain that the children are going to try

## Focus of Learning
**To learn, recite and act out poems to express preferences in poetry, giving reasons**

to write their own humorous poem. One of the funniest types of poems is the limerick. The limerick is a five-line poem in which the first, second and fifth lines rhyme and have a specific special rhythm. Show the children a few examples and discuss.

- Tell the class that there is going to be a competition in which they must work in small groups, pick a humorous poem, and then learn, recite and perform the poem in front of the class. The winning poem will get a prize. Give the children a certain amount of time to practise and at the end of the lesson they all perform their poems.

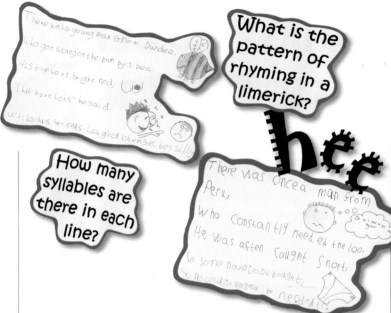

## Practical Activities

- In small groups, invite the children to write their own limerick poem.
- Play 'Lost Lines'. Present the children with a selection of limerick poems with missing lines. In pairs, ask the children to attempt to write the missing lines.
- Give the children a large selection of humorous poems and ask them to classify the poems according to their type. Ask them to select one poem from each type and write what they like and don't like about that particular poem.
- Make a class humorous poetry book. Ask the children to choose their own favourite humorous poem to write and illustrate and explain why they like it.

## Display Ideas

- Paint and collage a giant laughing mouth for display.
- Ask the children to illustrate their own limerick poems as well as original limerick poems.

- Make a collage of laughing faces from magazines and newspapers. Ask the children to type a humorous poem of their choice to display on the collage.
- Create a shape poem using vocabulary associated with laughter and humour; for example, giggle, chuckle, chortle.

## Cross-curricular Links

- **PSHCE** – 'A day without laughter is a day wasted' – discuss. Ask the children what makes them laugh, why do people laugh, what occasions make them laugh?
- **Literacy** – Read and share a selection of jokes and make your own class joke book.
- **Drama** – Ask the children to dramatise a limerick.

# Haiku Poetry

## Whole-class Starter

- In role, enter the class as a very studious literary type of character. Explain that you are going to teach the children about 'proper' poetry, poetry from another country. The poetry they are going to learn about is very serious and is called 'haiku poetry' and it comes from Japan. Read and show the children a selection of haiku poems and ask them what they notice about the poems. Explain that haiku poetry has three lines – the first line and third line have five syllables and the middle line has seven.

- Explain that in order to write such great poetry, the children need to know what a syllable is. Tell them that a syllable is a single unit of sound within a word and give an example. Ask the children to work with a partner, and from out of your 'very sensible' briefcase, pull a laminated

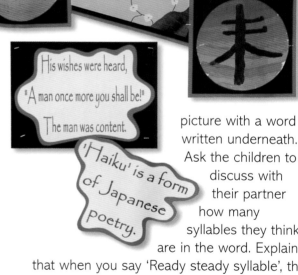

picture with a word written underneath. Ask the children to discuss with their partner how many syllables they think are in the word. Explain that when you say 'Ready steady syllable', they should hold up the correct number of fingers for syllables. Check their responses and repeat several times. Deal with any misconceptions.

**Focus of Learning**
To develop an understanding of poetry from other cultures
To identify syllables within words

- Play 'Hunt the Haiku'. Prepare a set of laminated A4 sheets with several examples of haiku poetry. Ensure that only one of them is a correct haiku, the others should contain mistakes, such as four lines instead of three, too many syllables or not enough syllables. Divide the children into small groups and give each group a sheet of poems. Together the children must look at the poems and hunt for the one which is the haiku. Discuss their responses. Once they have established which poem is the haiku, they must guess what the haiku is about.

- Explain that now they know what a haiku poem is and have read lots, they must try to write one. From your briefcase pull out an object, such as a toy frog or an apple. Challenge the children to work in pairs to write a haiku about that object. For example:

  *Hop on lilypad,*
  *Catching flies with its long tongue,*
  *Green and warty skin.*

## Practical Activities

- Read the story *The Stonecutter (various versions available on the internet, e.g. www. pitt.edu/~dash/japan.html).* Explain this story is a well-known Japanese folk tale. The children listen carefully to the story and in small groups write a haiku that tells the story.
- Read a selection of haiku poetry and ask the children to notice other features; for example, haiku poems rarely rhyme. Can they find a rhyming haiku.
- Play 'Hidden Haiku'. Make a set of haiku poems about a variety of everyday objects or fairy tales. Slice the poems up and place them into a feely box. Give each child in the group the object or fairy-tale picture. The children take turns to pick out a line of a haiku and decide if it belongs to their object or fairy tale. The first person to make a complete and correct haiku wins the game.
- Look at a selection of different types of poems that have a strict form; for example, haiku, limerick, riddle, cinquain.

## Display Ideas

- Colour mix a sunset background using yellow, red and orange powder paint. Research Japanese symbols and paint a chosen symbol in black on the sunset background.
- Look at artwork based around the Japanese blossom tree. Using blue paper, black paint and pink paper recreate a blossom tree design.
- Make a clay tile and either recreate a blossom tree design on the tile or a Japanese symbol.

Hidden Haikus

Hidden Haiku

Hidden Haikus

Sold his cow for beans

Up and up he climbed

Grew into a big beanstalk

Hidden Haiku

Hidden Haiku

Hidden Haiku

Hidden Haikus

Hidden Haiku

Hidden Haikus

Hidden Haikus

## Cross-curricular Links

- **Geography** – Locate on a world map or globe the location of Japan. Learn about the cultures and traditions of this Far Eastern country.
- **Literacy** – Ask the children to write their own version of *The Stonecutter* folk tale, adding in other things he might wish to be.
- **Literacy** – Read a selection of other Japanese folk tales and compare with traditional tales from other cultures.

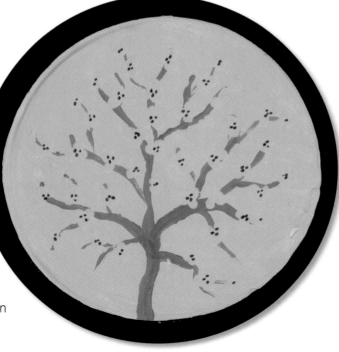

# Pandora's Box

A MYTH EXPLORES THE RELATIONSHIP BETWEEN GOD AND HUMANS.

IN MANY MYTHS, HUMANS DISOBEY THE GODS.

AN ORIGIN MYTH EXPLAINS THE BEGINNING OF SOMETHING.

PANDORA'S BOX IS AN ORIGIN MYTH.

THERE ARE MANY MYTHS ACROSS MANY CULTURES.

A MYTH TRIES TO EXPLAIN WHY THE WORLD IS AS IT IS.

HOPE

Pandora's Box

GREED  POVERTY  FEAR  IDLENESS  ANGER  SELFISHNE

CRUELTY  DISEASE  HATRED  JEALOUSY

## Whole-class Starter

- Using a selection of props with the help of the children, retell the story of Pandora's Box. from *Orchard Book of Greek Myths* by Geraldine Mccaughrean (Orchard Books) Discuss what happened in the story and what the story was trying to teach us. Make it clear that this story is a Greek myth. The Greeks created myths as a way of explaining things about the world that were difficult to understand. This story tries to show us why there are such horrible things in our world. In Greek myths things often happen as a result of somebody disobeying the Greek gods.

- Explain that Pandora's Box is a Greek origin myth, this means it describes the beginning of something; for example, how evil things in

## Focus of Learning
**To learn about the features of a myth**

the world began. Tell the children that they are going to explore various myths and see what each one is trying to describe. Ask them to work in small groups and give each group a simplified version of a Greek myth to read and discuss. Recall the groups, and as a whole class make a list of the different myths, their main characters and similarities and differences. Explain that all myths have similar features, such as gods often appear in myths, myths attempt to explain the world, myths are not based on truth.

- In a large classroom space or hall, ask the

children to think about the story and envisage what came out of the box. Explain that lots of versions of the story have been written and they all describe the contents of Pandora's Box in a different way. For example, Hope was described as a dove in one story but a dragonfly in another and a magical creature in another story. Ask the children to work individually or small groups to create a motif that depicts Hope and 'the spites that trouble mankind'. Encourage them to call out words that relate to their motif. Discuss their choice of motif.

- Discuss with the children how the story of Pandora's Box considers things that trouble mankind. Ask if there was a box in our school, what would we want to keep locked up inside that might trouble our school; for example, unkind children. Give each child a piece of paper and a pencil. Ask them to write what they would like to put in the school's Pandora's Box and place their suggestions in an actual box. Ask the children to sit in a circle and, one at a time, they open the box and reveal what others have said. Discuss their responses.

out the myth. Each group could perform their myth to the class.
- Prepare a set of laminated charts that list the features of a Greek myth. Using the Greek myths from the carpet session, ask the children to read and complete their chart by identifying the mythical features of their story.

## Display Ideas

- Ask the children to imagine and draw one of the 'spites that trouble mankind' that came out of Pandora's Box.
- Paint and collage a large image of Hope.
- Draw and watercolour one of the Greek gods.

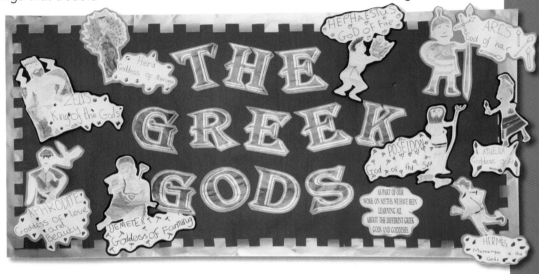

Include emblems in the picture to illustrate what he or she is god of; for example, Zeus might be carrying a thunderbolt.
- Sculpt a Greek vase using clay. Paint and decorate the vase using Greek symbol.

## Practical Activities

- Ask the children to make their own Pandora's Box using the net of a cube. Decorate the box using Greek symbols. Ask the children to draw pictures to represent the other good things there are in the world apart from hope, such as love, family, friendship.
- Research the Greek gods and create a booklet entitled 'Gallery of Gods'.
- In small groups, give each group a different Greek myth. Ask the children to use props to act

## Cross-curricular Links

- **Literacy** – Ask the children to write their own Greek myth explaining why there is evil in the world.
- **Maths** – Explore the nets of other solid shapes, such as cuboid, pyramid, cylinder, triangular prism.

# King Midas

## Whole-class Starter

● Make a set of large picture cards that tell the story of King Midas. Place the pictures on the board. In pairs, ask the children to discuss what they think is happening in each picture. Taking a picture at a time, invite the children to tell you what they think happened in the story of King Midas. Scribe simple information below each picture.

  ● Explain that being an oral storyteller is not just about being able to tell stories. A storyteller needs to be able to captivate the audience because they don't have pictures to help them convey the story. A storyteller must use the correct language, use different voices, project their voice and create a magical atmosphere full of suspense. Prepare two recordings that tell the story of King Midas. Ensure the two recordings are different. For example, one story should be quite simple and basic, while the other should be full of elaborate language that excites the children and brings the story

## Focus of Learning
**To learn about the tradition of oral storytelling**
**To retell the story orally using story language**

to life. Ask the children to listen to both recordings and as a class discuss what they notice about the two stories. Which story do they prefer and why?

● Make a selection of A4 pictures that are quite detailed. Ask the children to work in small groups to discuss what is happening in the picture. Together they must decide how best to describe the picture using oral language. Invite each group to orally tell the rest of the class what is happening in their picture. Show the picture to the class and discuss whether or not they could add any more exciting language.

● Give the children a very simple version of King Midas. Make a recording of the same story.

Ask the children to read their story and then listen to the recorded story. Discuss with them the differences between the written and the oral versions. Make a shopping list of things they might use when they are retelling a story, such as voices for different characters, sound effects, speed of voice, pause for effect, moments of silence, use of language, repetition.

## Practical Activities

● Give each group another Greek myth in pictorial form. Ask them to work together to retell the story orally. Record each group telling their version of the story. At the end of the session, listen to each other's stories and discuss similarities and differences.

● In small groups, give the children a written version of a myth and a gold pen. Explain that you would like them to give their story the golden touch. They must read the story together and pick out the bits where it would be most appropriate for them to use some of the story techniques they have learned, such as a part of the story where it would be good to use sound effects, or use a slow dramatic voice.

● Play 'Surprise Stories'. Sit the children in a circle. Make a selection of words or pictures and place them in a box. Each child picks out a word but must keep it a secret. The object of the game is to tell a story but the children must include the word that they have taken from the box. Each child takes it in turn to tell their part of the story and include their word or picture in the story.

● Buy a selection of pre-recorded stories for the children to listen to. Ask the children to listen to them and as a group discuss their favourite story. Encourage them to explain why they liked the story so much.

## Display Ideas

● Ask the children to draw and paint pictures of gold objects that King Midas has touched and they have turned to gold.
● Draw and paint a picture of King Midas and his palace.
● Ask the children to draw a scene from the story of King Midas. Put the drawings together to create a pictorial representation of the King Midas story.

● Explain that in the story King Midas thought that turning things to gold would make him happy but in fact it made him very miserable. Using the idea of gold, ask the children what golden rules would make our class or school a happy or better place. Invite the children to illustrate them. Create a class 'golden rules' board.

## Cross-curricular Links

● **PSHCE** – Explore other greedy characters in fiction and how they learned their lessons.
● **Science** – Investigate changing materials from one state to another, such as water to ice or making jelly.
● **ICT** – Invite the children to take photographs of things around the school. Download them onto the computer and give them the Midas touch by turning them gold. Display as a 'before' and 'after' effect.

# King Arthur

## Whole-class Starter

- Explain that the children are going to learn about a group of stories called legends. Place the word *legend* on the interactive whiteboard and ask what a legend is. Explain that a legend is somebody who is so good at something that they have become legendary. For example, they will be remembered forever. Show the children pictures of possible legends; for example, David Beckham, Jonny Wilkinson, Marilyn Monroe. Discuss that stories called legends have a real hero at the centre of the story and are usually based on a true event in the past. However, they have often been embellished and changed over time with special 'mythical features'.

- Explain that the children are going to learn about one of the most famous legends of all time – a real king called King Arthur. Ask them to discuss with a partner what they know

### Focus of Learning
### To learn about the features of a legend

about this legend. Write any ideas they might have on the board. Retell the story in their own words. To add stimulus you could use props, pictures or a magic cloak that takes the children to Camelot.

- After listening to the story, ask the children to think about the features of a legend. Place these features on the board; for

example, based on a true event, a long time ago, often set in fantastic places, real hero at the centre of the story, special mythical features, important meaning for a culture or religion. Discuss the features in relation to the story of King Arthur and establish which bits of the story are likely and which are embellished. For example, it is likely that Arthur became king but Excalibur rising out of the lake is an embellishment.

- Play 'Table Trivia'. Using a multimedia package, create a circle to represent the Round Table. Prepare a presentation that enables names or keywords from the story to flash on to the table. Give each child a laminated circle (to represent the Round Table) and a whiteboard pen. When a name or keyword flashes on the screen, the children explain the relevance of that person or event on their laminated table. For example, if the word Excalibur appears, they could write, 'The sword that rose from the lake'.

## Practical Activities

- In small groups, read and share the book *King Arthur and the Knights of the Round Table* by Marcia Williams (Walker Books).
- Give each child a circular piece of paper to represent the Round Table. Ask them to select their favourite modern-day heroes who they think may one day become legendary. Using the computer, print out a picture of their face, turn it into a knight and place on their Round Table.
- Ask the children to take a modern-day event; for example, Jonny Wilkinson kicking the winning goal for the England rugby team

to win the World cup. Ask them to retell this event in the style of a legend, such as using story language, change the setting to something fantastic, add in some mythical features and embellish some of the details.
- Ask the children to sit in small groups and read other legends such as Robin Hood, George and the Dragon, Odysseus. Discuss with them the features of legends and how they relate to the stories they are reading.

## Display Ideas

- Using the book *King Arthur and the Knights of the Round Table* as a stimulus, ask the children to use the front cover to give them ideas about what the knights looked like in order to draw and colour their own knight.
- Invite the children to collage their own shield that symbolises their own personality and interest. For example, a child who likes art may collage a paintbrush and pallet.
- Ask the children to paint and collage shields that belong to each knight of the Round Table.
- Paint and collage a large jousting knight using the illustrations from the book as a stimulus.

## Cross-curricular Links

- **History** – Research the knights of the Round Table. What can they discover about the life of a knight? Why did knights have different shields or emblems? What strengths and weaknesses did the knights possess?
- **PSHCE** – Discuss with the children the qualities of a knight. What qualities do people need to posses in order to be a knight? Discuss receiving a knighthood. Do you need the same or different qualities today?
- **Outdoor adventure activity** – Taking the idea from the story of the challenge that was presented to Arthur to remove the stone from the rock. Present the children with a variety of OAA that will offer them problem-solving challenges.

# Robin Hood

## Whole-class Starter

- Tell the class that they are going to learn about the legend of Robin Hood. Ask the children what they know about legends. Discuss the features of a legend with them (see 'King Arthur', pages 42–43). Read to the class the first chapter of *The Adventures of Robin Hood* by Marcia Williams (Walker Books), entitled 'Robin of Locksley becomes an outlaw'. Working in pairs with one copy of *The Adventures of Robin Hood* per pair, ask the children to read and discuss chapters two to four.

- Recall the children and tell them that you have placed large sheets of paper around the room with chapter one, two, three and four written across the top. Give the children a set of sticky notes or ask them to write on the paper what has happened

## Focus of Learning
### To respond imaginatively to what they have read

in each chapter. Encourage them to write down important facts about the events and characters in each chapter. Discuss their responses.

- Sit the children in a circle. In the middle, place pictures of the main characters and places from the story of Robin Hood; for example, Friar Tuck, Sherwood Forest, Sheriff of Nottingham, Maid Marian, Little John, Robin Hood, King Richard, Merry Men. Pass a big feather around the circle while singing or listening to the Robin Hood song (theme from TV series *The Adventures of Robin Hood* 1955–60, Carl Sigman). At the end of the song or when the music stops, whoever has the feather must pick up a picture and tell the class something about that place or character. For example, a child might select the Sheriff of Nottingham and say 'In league with Prince John' or they might select King Richard and say 'Away fighting the crusades.' Encourage the children to think about what they have read in the text.

- Explain that Robin Hood had lots of adventures and today the children's challenge is to write a new adventure for him. To ensure that they stay faithful to the legend of Robin Hood, they must remember that their story must solve a problem in which Robin saves the day. To get the children thinking, place a few problems on the board that Robin could be faced with. Ask the children to discuss with a partner possible ways in which Robin could save the day; for example, Maid Marian is kidnapped, how might Robin rescue her?

## Practical Activities

- Plan and write a new adventure for Robin Hood. Type up the adventures and print on parchment-style coloured paper.
- Ask the children to choose a character from the story. They must draw and colour their character. They should annotate their drawing with words to describe their character and quotes from the text.
- Using the characters from the carpet session, place a large target on the wall. In a bag, place words or phrases from the text that describe the characters. The children pick a word or phrase, and then using Velcro® balls or arrows, they must try to hit their character. Give each child five lives and if they miss they lose a life. The winner is the child who has the most lives at the end of the game.
- Ask the children to invent a new character for the legend of Robin

Hood. Discuss with them what type of character might make the Robin Hood adventures even better. Is their character going to be a hero or a villain? Male or female? Has the character got a particular strength or weakness? How is the character introduced in to the story? What effect might the character have on other characters?

## Display Ideas

- Collage and paint a large Robin Hood shooting his arrow.
- Ask the children to draw and colour leaves, arrows, acorns that can be cut out and used as a border on the display.
- Sponge a tree and place words relating to the story around and on the tree. This can be used when writing to help the children to locate their keywords.
- Based on the statue of Robin Hood at Nottingham Castle, ask the children to sculpt their own Robin Hood statue out of clay.

## Cross-curricular Links

- **Environmental Science** – Ask the children to become a 'tree detective' for the day. Ask them to take pictures of trees within the school grounds. Collect leaves and fruit from each tree. Use books to identify what type of tree it is. Make labels for each tree that include facts about the tree and how it changes through the seasons.
- **Outdoor Adventure Activity** – Offer the children an experience of archery.

# The Lion and the Mouse

## Whole-class Starter

- Read and enjoy the story 'Lion and the Mouse' in *Aesop's Funky Fables* by Vivian French and Korky Paul (Puffin Books). Stop during reading to discuss the illustrations. Ask the children what the first picture tells them about the characters in the story. Why do they think the lion lets the mouse go? What happens to the lion in the story? How does the mouse help him? What is the moral of the fable? Finally, ask what the last picture tells about the characters in the story.

- Place a large picture of the lion and the mouse on the board. Ask the children to work with a partner to discuss the characteristics of the two animals. Invite the children to share their ideas. Write them on the board next to or around the characters. Explain that Aesop wrote lots of fables and most of them had animals in them. Tell the children they are going to investigate the types of animals that Aesop used and their characteristics. In small groups, give the children a fable to read. Ensure that different fables are used but try to include those that have similar animals; for example, 'The Boy who cried Wolf', 'The Wolf and the Crane', 'The Fox and the Crow' and 'the Fox and the Stork'.

## Focus of Learning
**To learn about the different types of characters in a fable**

- Place around the room pictures of the different characters from the fables that the children have read. Give the children some sticky notes and ask them to write words to describe the characters and put these on the appropriate picture. At the end of the session, collect all the pictures and discuss the children's responses. Draw attention to a character that appears in several stories. Discuss whether the character is always the same or different in each story; for example, is the wolf ever a good character?

- Play 'Character Conundrum'. In a large space or hall, place between six and eight mats around the room. On each mat, put a picture of an animal from one of Aesop's fables. Prepare a dice with words

In 'The Lion and T Mouse' I am kind when I help the lion.

that are characteristics of the animals; for example, *foolish*, *sly*, *helpful*, *kind*. Explain that the children must move around the room to jungle sounds or music and when the music stops they must stand on or next to a mat of their choice. Roll the dice and whatever characteristic it lands on, if their animal displays that feature, they are out of the game and must sit in a 'waiting pen'. The winner of the game is the person who stays 'in' the longest.

## Practical Activities

- Ask the children to draw a cartoon strip telling the fable of the lion and the mouse.
- Make some laminated characters typical of fables and place in a bag or box. Ask the children to pick two characters out of the box and write a fable about them. Present in an animal-shaped booklet.
- Ask the children to work in pairs and choose two contrasting characters to draw and annotate by using similes to describe their characteristics; for example, 'as helpful as a nurse', 'as mean as a wicked witch'.
- Play 'Aesop's Bingo'. Make a selection of bingo boards that contain words describing the characteristics of the characters from Aesop's fables. Make each board different. Make a spinner that has pictures of characters from Aesop's fables (an eight spinner would be good). Give each child a board. The children take turns to spin the spinner. Whichever animal they land on, they must cover a word on

their board that corresponds with that animal. The object of the game is to cover all the words on the bingo board.

## Display Ideas

- Paint and collage large animals from a variety of favourite Aesop's fables.
- Research the work of Henri Rousseau (1844–1910) and look closely at his material based on the jungle. Ask the children to recreate his work using a selection of mediums, such as watercolours, pastels, ICT paint package.
- On a circled piece of blue hessian, recreate one of Rousseau's jungle scenes using a variety of green materials and threads.
- Take a photo of each of the children's faces. Stick the photograph in the middle of a piece of A4 paper. Ask the children to pick a character from a fable and turn themselves into that animal by drawing the animal around their face.

## Cross-curricular Links

- **History** – Research the life of Aesop and write a rhyming biography or an epitaph.
- **Science** – Ask the children to choose their favourite animal from a fable and research that particular animal. Create a factfile or multimedia presentation that tells us facts and features about your particular animal. Focus on habitat, food, physical characteristics, etc.
- **Music** – Discuss the type of sound or music that the children think would represent a particular character at a particular point in the story, such as the hare snoozing under the tree, the aggressive lion, the helpful mouse chewing on the rope. Ask the children to compose their own sounds. They could then compose a sound track to accompany the retelling of a fable.

# The Hare and the Tortoise

## Whole-class Starter

- Explain that the children are going to read a special kind of story called a fable. Using the word *fable*, write an acrostic poem that identifies the key features of a fable. For example:
  - **F** ew characters
  - **A** nimals
  - **B** rief tales
  - **L** esson learned
  - **E** nd has a moral
- Tell the children that you are going to read a fable called 'The Hare and the Tortoise' by Aesop (*Aesop's Funky Fables* by Vivian French and Korky Paul, Puffin Books). Explain that this story has a moral because it is a fable. Ask them to listen to the story and try to identify the moral.
- Present the children with a picture of the hare and a picture of the tortoise on the board.

### Focus of Learning
**To identify typical story themes in fables**

Ask why they think these characters are used and what are their main characteristics. Discuss that the hare is often used in fables as a foolish character. Ask the children if they can think of two other characters that could be used instead of the hare and the tortoise. Encourage them to think of characters appropriate to different settings; for example, jelly fish and shark, or cheetah and African snail.

- Prepare a selection of short fables for the children to read. Ask them to work with a partner. Give each pair a fable to read together and decide what they think the moral of the story could be. On the board, show a selection of morals. Invite the children to choose what they think is the correct moral to their story.

● Play 'Muddled Morals'. Give each pair a whiteboard and pen. On the board, place a jumbled up moral and ask the children to correctly write the moral on their whiteboard; for example, 'steady and race wins the slow' would be 'slow and steady wins the race'.

## Practical Activities

● Invite the children to write their own fable. Present it in an animal-shaped booklet.

● Prepare a selection of fables (try to choose fables that the children have not already heard). In small groups, give each child in the group the same fable to read. On a whiteboard, ask the children to write what they think the moral is. The children reveal and discuss their answers. Reveal the true moral to the children and together compare the answers.

● Present a selection of books and stories. These must include fables and non-fables. Ask the children to work in a group to sort the stories and books into fables and non-fables. Discuss their choices.

● In small groups, read the children a fable and ask them to design a front cover to a new book that illustrates the story theme.

● Taking the word *tortoise*, ask the children to rewrite the story using the letters from the word tortoise to start each sentence. For example:

– **T** ortoise and hare had an argument
– **O** ver who was the quickest
– **R** ace you said Hare
– **T** ortoise agreed
– **O** n your marks get set go!
– **I** n a flash Hare ran away
– **S** lowly tortoise overtook hare
– **E** verybody cheered because tortoise won the race

## Display Ideas

● Paint and collage a large hare and tortoise for display.

● Ask the children to paint an animal that could be watching the race.

● Paint giant tortoises and ask the children to write their own acrostic poem of fables on each section of the tortoises' shell.

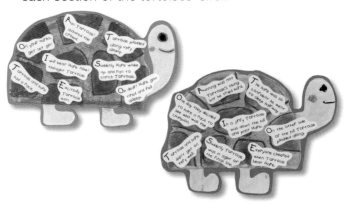

● Make a clay tortoise using small stones to create the shell effect.

● Make tortoise and hare puppets.

● Ask the children to paint pictures to illustrate opposites.

● Using a block printing technique, ask the children to work with a partner to create a tile that illustrates opposites.

## Cross-curricular Links

● **Literacy** – Use the story as a stimulus for exploring opposites. Introduce the children to the word *antonyms*.

● **PSHCE** – Discuss with the children the moral in the story and the importance of determination and how showing off is not a very good quality.

● **Physical Education** – Organise a sports day or an afternoon of fun-filled races based around the hare and the tortoise fable.

# The Magic Key

## Whole-class Starter

- Read and enjoy one of the Magic Key stories by Roderick Hunt and Alex Brychta (Oxford University Press). Ask the children to think about the story and the adventure that Biff, Chip and Kipper embark on. Ask what these characters were doing at the beginning of the story, what signalled the beginning of the adventure, what did their adventure consist of and what signalled the end of their adventure.

- Read and enjoy the second book in the series, *Pirate Adventure*. Discuss the similarities between the two stories. For example, the beginning of the story is always a clue to the adventure, the magic key always glows, whoever is present at the time goes on the adventure, the children always bring back a souvenir.

## Focus of Learning
To draw on knowledge and experience of text in deciding and planning what and how to write adventure stories

- Explain that the children are going to be 'adventure analysts'. Ask them to work in small mixed-ability groups, possibly with an adult. Give each group a Magic Key adventure book to read. Ask the children to read the story and check if their story has similar features to *The Magic Key* and *Pirate Adventure*. Ask each group to give feedback to the class.

- Play 'Add an Adventure'. This game is based on the idea of 'I went to market and bought…'.

Sit the children in a circle and ask one child to begin the adventure by saying 'The magic key glowed and took me to…'. The next person repeats 'The magic key glowed and took me to … and …'. The children must remember the adventure and add to the adventure. When a mistake is made, they must start again! The idea for this game is to encourage the children to think of lots of different adventures.

## Practical Activities

- Ask the children to write and illustrate their own new adventure for the Magic Key series.
- Collect a selection of small objects and place them in the box. Explain that each object in the box is a souvenir bought back from an adventure. In small groups, the children pick out an object, discuss a possible adventure and create a small play that explains how the object got in the box. The children perform their mini adventures to the group.
- Give the children a selection of pictures from one of the adventures that they would not have read. Mix up the pictures and ask the group to organise the pictures into what they think are the correct order. On large pieces of paper, ask the children to work together to write the adventure. Encourage them to model their language on the story books.
- Give each child in the group a different Magic Key book. Ask them to look at the back of the book to see which keywords are taught in this book. Give some ideas and ask the children to design and make a board game to reinforce these keywords.

## Display Ideas

- Draw, paint and collage the characters from the Magic Key story.
- Ask the children to use chalk pastels to illustrate possible settings for new Magic Key adventures.
- Using the idea from the story in which the characters or objects get bigger and smaller. Ask the children to draw a picture that relates to an aspect of the story; for example, key, Biff, Floppy. Enlarge and reduce the pictures using a photocopier. Ask the children to cut out the different-sized pictures and create a

collage of their object. The pictures could be kept black and white or invite the children to use pencil crayons to colour their picture.

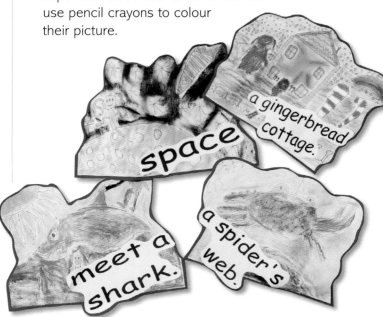

- Collect together a selection of old and new keys. Ask the children to use specialist sketching pencils or charcoal and their observational skills to draw in detail a variety of different shaped keys.

## Cross-curricular Links

- **D&T** – Design and make an adventure board game based around one of the Magic Key adventures.
- **Maths** – Focus on the concept of larger than, smaller than, bigger than, etc.
- **ICT** – In small groups, ask the children to work together to create a new adventure. Using a paint package, ask each child to draw a page for each part of the story.

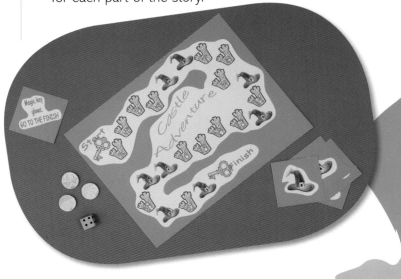

# Whatever Next!

Whatever Next!

We have been reading the story 'Whatever Next' by Jill Murphy.

We read the story both with and without punctuation.

We talked about how the punctuation helps the reader.

Punctuation gives the reader clues to help them read the story.

## Whole-class Starter

- Read and enjoy the story *Whatever Next!* by Jill Murphy (Macmillan Children's Books). Discuss the adventure that Baby Bear has just been on and what he used to take him on his adventure. Present a selection of objects and ask the children to take turns to choose an object and say what type of adventure they would go on and how they would use the object; for example, 'This is not a stick, it is a magic wand and I am a magician in a travelling circus.'

Punctuation gives the reader clues to help them read the story.

### Focus of Learning
**To learn how punctuation gives the reader clues to help them read a story with some variety of pace and emphasis**

- Reread the story but ignore all the punctuation. For example, read without stopping, don't use voices, don't use any inflection for questions, etc. Ask the children what they notice about the way you have read the text. Explain that you read without taking notice of the punctuation the author has used. Ask the children what they think punctuation is. Make a list of the different types of punctuation that they know and discuss.
- Give each pair a section of the story to read.

Ask them to identify the punctuation in each section and explain what the punctuation is telling the reader to do. Also discuss any text in capital letters or italics. Encourage each pair to give feedback to the class.

● On the interactive whiteboard, show a big picture from another of Jill Murphy's stories, *Peace at Last* (Macmillan Children's Books). Underneath the picture should be the accompanying text but with the punctuation missing. Ask the children to work in pairs and give each pair a whiteboard and pen. Ask them to discuss with their partner what punctuation the author might use and why and copy the piece of text, adding the punctuation that they think would be appropriate. Discuss their ideas and then reveal the real text and the punctuation used by the author.

## Practical Activities

● Give a small group the story *Peace at Last* or another Jill Murphy text and ask them to work as a group to practise reading the text aloud, using the punctuation as clues to help them add a variety of pace, emphasis and expression.

● Play 'Punctuation Pandemonium'. Type out the text from the story *Whatever Next!* including the correct punctuation and laminate. Make a spinner that has on each side a type of punctuation that is in the text and a picture of a rocket and a star. The children should spin the spinner and if it points to a piece of punctuation, they should circle one example of it on their board. If it points to the rocket, they can circle one of each piece of punctuation but if it points to the star, they must rub their board clean! The person at the end with the most pieces of punctuation circled is the winner.

● Play 'Punctuation Pelmanism'. Make two sets of cards in two different colours. One set should show punctuation marks from the story and the other should show a sentence or phrase from the story in which the

punctuation is missing. The children should take turns to turn over a card of each colour. If the punctuation mark matches the punctuation missing from the text, they can keep that pair; if not, they put the cards back. The winner is the person with the most cards at the end.

● Using the ideas from the carpet session, the children choose an object from the box and write their own adventure story about their object.

## Display Ideas

● Paint and collage Baby Bear and Owl from the picnic scene. Add real picnic items onto the scene for a 3D effect.

● Ask the children to think about their own adventure stories, and using the illustrator's style as a stimulus, create two pictures, one in black and white and one in colour, depicting part of their story.

● Chalk pastel Baby Bear in various poses from the story.

● Use white chalks on black paper to create Baby Bear in a box soaring over the rooftops.

## Cross-curricular Links

● **Science** – Learn all about space, the planets and the solar system. Create a factual space display entitled 'Soar into Space'.

● **D&T** – Design and make 3D models of the solar system, or using recyclable materials, ask the children to create a 3D rocket.

● **PSHCE** – Create a class bear that gets taken home weekly by a different class member. The bear has a diary in which children must write or draw what the bear has been up to!

speech marks

question mark

What colour is the sun?

Punctuation Pelmanism

**53**

# A Dark, Dark Tale

## Whole-class Starter

- Read and enjoy the story *A Dark, Dark Tale* by Ruth Brown (Red Fox). Stop at the point where the book reads 'In the corner was a dark, dark box'. Tell the children that the box is opening and ask what they think might be inside. Before revealing the answer, explain that this type of story is known as a mystery story because it keeps the reader guessing about what is going to happen at the end of the story. Throughout a mystery story there should be some clues to help them solve the mystery. Invite the children to look back through the book to try to find clues about what could be in the box.

## Focus of Learning
**To introduce the children to the genre of mystery stories**

- Scan the pictures in the book onto a computer and display on an interactive whiteboard. Show the children one picture at a time. Ask them to discuss with a partner any clues they can see in the picture. Invite them to circle things in the picture that they think are clues to the mystery 'What is in the box?' The children will notice lots of things hidden in the picture but eventually they will notice that in most of the pictures there is a cat and this is a crucial clue to what lies in the box. At the end of this, reveal the answer. Explain that often mystery stories have surprise endings, a twist in the tale – do they think that this ending was a surprise? What will happen next?

- Explain that mystery stories always build a sense of tension throughout the book. Explain what this means. For example, the book gets more and more exciting and tense until the reader reaches the climax of the story, which is the most exciting part. Reread the story and ask the children to think about how the author builds the tension, such as the use of repetitive language, travelling deeper and deeper into the house into smaller spaces. Also ask the children to identify the climax of the story.

- Play 'It's a Mystery'. Write six mystery stories using the same format as *A Dark, Dark Tale* but using different settings. For example:
  *Once upon a time there was a dark, dark village.*
  *In the village there was a dark, dark street.*
  *On the street there was a dark, dark school.*
  *In the school there was a dark, dark corridor.*
  *At the end of the corridor there was a dark,*
       *dark door.*
  *Behind the dark, dark door was a …*

- Cut the stories into six parts and place them in an envelope. Ask the children to get into groups of six and give each group an envelope. The children must organise the sentences into the correct order using their knowledge of mystery stories. Ask them to complete the end of the mystery story. While they are sorting their sentences, play the song 'It's a Mystery' by Toyah Wilcox. Invite each group to read their mystery story to the class revealing the hidden mystery.

## Practical Activities

- Ask the children to design a front cover for their own mystery story.

- Ask the children to draw and watercolour the illustrations from the book on A3 paper. Use these pictures for a display and ask the children to write the text that corresponds with the illustrations. On the display, don't include the final picture but replace it with the question 'What do you think is in the box?' Include on the display the features of a mystery story.

- Draw and chalk pastel pictures of the black cat in different poses.

- Ask the children to draw and pencil crayon

their own setting. The children should hide ten animals that could be camouflaged within the setting of their picture. Encourage the children to think about the setting and the animals they decide to hide. Laminate the pictures and ask the children to swap pictures with each other and try to locate the hidden objects.

## Display Ideas

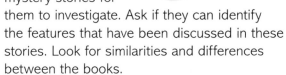

- Using the ideas from the carpet session, invite the children to write and illustrate their own mystery story. Encourage them to use the same format as the book and choose clues to add to their illustrations. Discuss how authors of mystery stories often use 'red herrings' to try to trick the reader. For example, Ruth Brown adds other things to her illustrations that are not relevant to the solution.

- Provide the children with a selection of mystery stories for them to investigate. Ask if they can identify the features that have been discussed in these stories. Look for similarities and differences between the books.

- Make a treasure hunt in which the children solve clues to find hidden letters around the school. Once they have found all the letters, they unscramble them to solve an anagram. The last clue leads them to a box where the solution or correct word is found.

- Make a simple mystery board game based on the same format as Cludeo in order that children practise solving clues to work out the solution to a mystery.

## Cross-curricular Links

- **Literacy** – Investigate words that contain the 'ar' phoneme.
- **D&T** – Using a shoebox, ask the children to work in small groups to design and make a house for a little mouse!
- **Geography** – Draw a map of the story and discuss geographical vocabulary, such as hill, wood, moor, river.

# A–Z Mysteries

## Whole-class Starter

- Explain that over the next week the children are going to investigate the genre of mystery stories. Look at a series of books titled *A to Z Mysteries* by Ron Roy (Random House). Explain that these books are based around a group of children called Dink, Ruth Rose and Josh – three young sleuths with a nose for adventure. The class are going to join these three on a mystery trail, pick up clues and see if they can help to solve a mystery and discover the features of a mystery story. Create with the children a mystery mind map that includes their ideas of what a mystery story entails. Explain that they need to check during the reading if they are right and if there are other features that might be added.

## Focus of Learning
**To learn about the features of a mystery story**

- Read chapters 1 and 2 to the children. Explain that mysteries are often like a puzzle. This particular story is a detective story with a dramatic event at the start and the mystery built around discovering 'whodunnit'. Explain that as they are going to be detectives for the week, the children are going have their own detective pocket book. Ask them to work with a partner to decide what they think is the dramatic start to this mystery story. The writer of a mystery story drops clues and red herrings to keep the reader guessing. Do they think they have come across any clues so far? Ask the detectives to write any key facts or clues in their pocket books.
- Reread the bottom of page 29 – 'Who'd want to steal a canary, a cat, a parrot, and a rabbit?' 'I don't know,' Dink said. 'But we're going to

find out!' Ask the children to discuss with their partner how they would try to solve this mystery. Invite them to explain their ideas to the class. Read chapters 3 and 4. Discuss and compare their plan with that of the children in the story. Discuss the character of Mr Little. The children in the story clearly suspect him of being a villain. However, the fact that he did not accept the reward seems to disprove that. What do they think? Ask the children to write facts and hunches about Mr Little in their pocket books.

- Read chapter 5 and discuss what the children have found out. Ask them to record relevant facts in their pocket book. For example, what was stolen from whom? Where were the characters when the burglaries took place? Read chapter 6 and discuss why Officer Fallon cannot arrest Mr Little? Ask if the children have spotted any more clues in this chapter, and if so, what?

- Read chapter 7 and 8, but before reading chapter 9, discuss the fact that a mystery story normally has a final part that wraps up all the clues and answers unanswered questions. As detectives, ask the children to see if they can do this before the final chapter is read. Prepare a set of questions about the mystery and place them around the school on giant laminated magnifying glasses. For example, Ruth Rose's cat Tiger has not been found yet. Where do you think she is? How did you know that Mr Little was the clown from the circus? How do you think Mr Little knew that the upstairs bathroom window was open? How did the police know that Fred Little would break in to Mrs Davis's house that night? Ask the children to write the answers in their pocket books and discuss as a class. Finish by reading chapter 9. Discuss how the author uses the disappearance of Ruth Rose's cat as a 'red herring'!

## Practical Activities

- Draw the map of Green Lawn. Plot the places on the map that are relevant to the story.
- Create a frontpage newspaper report for the *Sunday Morning Gazette* based on this story. Ask the children to think of a snappy headline, add a picture and include some eyewitness accounts.

- Give the children the blurb from other A to Z mystery adventures and ask them to write their own mystery story using the same characters and setting.
- Create an alphabet of the features of a mystery story; for example A is for A problem that needs solving, B is for bad characters, C is for clues for the reader to solve, D is for detective work.

## Display Ideas

- Paint and collage the main characters from the story.
- Create a black and white cartoon strip that highlights the main events in the story.
- Create a pen and ink map of the children's own locality.
- Create a ransom note for one of the missing pets in the story. Use the idea of cutting out letters from newspapers and sticking them together to make a message.

## Cross-curricular Links

- **Geography** – Using a map, ask the children to work out the quickest route between two given places. Place the map on a coordinate grid and ask them to give you coordinates of different places. Introduce directional language to describe a route.
- **Drama** – Give the children the blurb from other A to Z mystery adventures and ask them to work in groups to make up a short play based on the blurb. Video each story and share with the class.
- **Literacy** – Investigate the phoneme *c*, and the alternative ways of writing this phoneme; for example, *ck* and *k*. Link this to the famous detective Jacques Clouseau!

57

# Alice in Wonderland

## Whole-class Starter

- Enter in role as Alice in Wonderland. Alice bounces into the classroom very excitedly to tell the story about her recent adventure. She explains that it was somewhat strange and she can't decide whether it was real or not. She tells the beginning of the story using props or visual aids, such as a pocket watch, a gold key, a bottle with 'drink me' label on. Tell the story up to the point where Alice is in the pool of tears.

- Alice explains that she has had so many strange things happened to her on her adventure that she couldn't possibly tell them all. She would really like to share her story with the children though, so she explains that she is going to split the class into groups and gives each group a prop that is connected with one part of her story, such as a teapot or a croquet

## Focus of Learning
### To understand the features of a fantasy story

mallet. She also gives each group a copy of the chapter related to their prop and asks them to work together to read and discuss what happened.

- Alice asks the children to share her adventures with the rest of the class. Each group tells their part of the story and explains the significance of their prop. Using the interactive whiteboard, Alice shows pictures and characters from the story and places them in the correct order while recapping verbally on the main points of the story.

● Finally Alice reveals that everybody thinks her story is so strange and bizarre that they have turned it into a special kind of book. She shows several different editions of the story. She explains that because it is such a strange story it is called a fantasy story and illustrates what a fantasy story is by pulling the different features of a fantasy story out of her bag, such as some magic, or an unbelievable setting. These features might be displayed on large laminated playing cards.

## Practical Activities

● Make a zigzag book that tells the adventures of Alice in Wonderland.
● Give the children a selection of props and ask them to write a new adventure for Alice in Wonderland. Possible props could be a bunch of flowers, a cauldron, wellington boots.
● Using the idea of the bottle with the label that says 'drink me', give the children a bottle-shaped booklet. Ask them to imagine what is in the bottle; for example, gooey liquid, big gobstopper, sparkly dust with magic stars in. The children must decide what Alice should do with the potion and what the label might say; for example, rub me, suck me, listen to me, sprinkle me. Finally the children must reveal what will happen to Alice if she obeys the instruction on the label; for example, she will become invisible, turn green, be able to read minds.
● Gather together a large selection of blurbs from a variety of fictional books. In a small group, the children must read the blurb and according to the criteria must decide if the book is a fantasy story or not.

● Design and make a 'mad hat' to wear to a class tea party. Look at a range of different hats for ideas and discuss materials they might use, such as recycled materials, papier mâché, Lego® with moving parts.

## Display Ideas

● Paint and collage large pictures of the characters from the story.
● Paint giant playing cards.
● Using drawing ink, ask the children to sketch the characters from the story after looking at the original black and white illustrations.
● Use papier mâché technique to make a teapot and saucer.

## Cross-curricular Links

● **D&T** – Ask the children to use a cardboard box with a hole cut out of the top to create their own imaginary underground world.
● **Food Technology** – Teach the children to make jam tarts.
● **Science** – Investigate materials that shrink and expand. Explore life above and below ground.
● **PE** – Learn to play croquet.

# Where the Wild Things Are

## Whole-class Starter

- Explain that the children are going to read a new story. However, when they share the story it is going to be slightly different because although this is a picture book, they are not going to be shown the pictures. Instead, they are to imagine the story in their heads by just listening to the language. Read the story to the children all the way through.
- Reread the story but this time ask the children to sit at their desks and give them a piece of A4 paper divided into six sections. Explain that the story will be reread to them and will stop at different sections. They should imagine and draw what the corresponding illustration would look like. For example, read the first page and ask them to draw the picture of the little boy in his wolf suit. Then ask them to draw a picture of his

## Focus of Learning
### To use language to imagine and recreate roles and experiences

bedroom once the forest had grown.
- Invite the children to share their illustrations and discuss the similarities and differences between them. Discuss their reasoning behind their choice of illustrations.
- In advance, select some phrases, words or pages from the story that use different language effects. For example, 'He

sailed off through night and day and in and out of weeks and almost over a year,' uses time language; 'They roared their terrible roars and gnashed their terrible teeth and rolled their terrible eyes,' uses repetition. Show these on the interactive whiteboard and ask the children to work with a partner to discuss how the author has used language for effect in the story.

- At the end of the session, reread the story and show the illustrations and discuss them with the children.

## Practical Activities

- Create a role-play area in which the children can recreate the story or invent a new world for Max to explore. Include a bedroom for Max, a wolf suit and a boat.
- Ask the children to work in small groups to make a puppet that they would find in Max's imaginary world. Give them a pre-made puppet of Max and ask them to recreate an adventure for him.
- Ask the children to draw their own bedroom in which an imaginary land has grown; for example, a desert island, a jungle, a circus.
- In a small group, give each child a copy of the text from the book and discuss its meaning. Is it real? Or is it a fantasy? For example, does a forest really grow in Max's room? Why does he decide to leave the wild things? Was he really away for over a year?

## Display Ideas

- Ask the children to paint and collage their own 'wild thing'.
- Taking the ideas from the carpet session, ask the children to draw in more detail and on a larger scale (A3) the six parts of the story. Use chalk pastels to create colour.
- Using the inside of the front cover for inspiration, ask the children to cut out and create a leaf collage.
- After sharing the illustrations with the children,

ask them to draw a 'wild thing' in close detail. Stick these together in a strip format (similar to the text) to create a group illustration in the style of the text.

- Using a variety of collage materials, ask the children to work in small groups to create a 3D scene from the book. Create the scene in a lid of a shoebox or similar. Join the scenes together to create the land of the wild things.

## Cross-curricular Links

- **Maths** – Investigate the language of time, such as days, hours, weeks, years.
- **PSHCE** – Discuss with the children mischief they might get up too and the consequences. How does it make them feel when they have been punished for being naughty. Read the book *What's Naughty?* by Hiawyn Oram and Adrian Reynolds (Hodder Children's Books).
- **Small world** – Recreate Max's imaginary world using a water tray full of plants, a boat and creatures to represent the 'wild things'.

We acted out the story and invented new worlds for Max to explore.

# Bill's New Frock

## Whole-class Starter

- Explain that throughout the week the children are going to focus on a book called *Bill's New Frock* by Anne Fine (Egmont Books). Ask them

to think about the title and what they think it is about. Read the blurb to the children and explain that they are going to focus on the character of Bill Simpson and how he feels about being a girl.

## Day 1

- Read chapter 1 'A really awful start'. Show the picture on page 2 (enlarged on the interactive whiteboard). Ask the children to work with a partner and give each pair a sticky note. Invite the children to think about words

that describe how Bill is feeling at this moment. Ask them to write the words on their sticky note and place it on the picture. Discuss why Bill feels like this and the differences between girls and boys.

- Ask the children to draw a picture of Bill in his new frock in the centre of a sheet of A3. Around the sheet add the other characters that Bill meets in the first chapter. Give each character a speech bubble and add quotes from the text that reflect how their attitude to Bill has changed now he is a girl.

### Focus of Learning
To study a character in depth and explore characters' feelings throughout a text

- Give each child a cut-out pair of jeans and a dress. Ask the children to think of adjectives that describe girls and boys. The children must write the appropriate adjectives on the dress and the jeans.

## Day 2

- Read chapter 2 'The Wumpy Choo' but stop at the end of page 21 where Bill says 'I'll do it'. Invite the children to think about what a Wumpy Choo looks like. Is it an animal and if so what type of animal could it be?
- Ask the children to draw or paint what they think the Wumpy Choo is.
- Using the letters from Wumpy Choo ask the children to write an acrostic poem to describe their Wumpy Choo. For example:

    *Woolly and hairy,*
    *Under a bush it lives,*
    *Magic powers,*
    *Poisonous sting,*
    *Yuk it smells*
    *Crawls along,*
    *Hates humans,*
    *Orange eyebrows,*
    *Oh no it's escaped!*

- Read the end of the chapter and discuss what a real Wumpy Choo is.

## Day 3

- Read chapter 3 'Pink, pink, nothing but pink'. Invite one of the boys to dress in Bill's new frock. Provide a pink dress, shoes and freckles. Ask the class why Mrs Collins chose Bill for the class to paint. Discuss how Bill felt and why? Arrange the class in a semicircle and sit Bill in the middle and ask him to adopt the embarrassed pose of Bill in the story. Invite each member of the class to say how they think Bill is feeling now.
    - While still in a semicircle, ask the children to paint Bill in his new frock.
- Ask them to be 'text detectives' and find evidence in the chapter of how Bill was feeling. Ask them to write direct quotes from the text around the picture, for example, 'There was no fight left in Bill Simpson.'

## Day 4

- Read chapter 4 'No pockets'. Explain that throughout this chapter Bill's feelings change quite dramatically. Show a timeline of the things that happen to Bill during this chapter. Give each pair a laminated pink dress and a whiteboard pen. Discuss what happens to Bill and ask the children to write how they think Bill feels at certain times in the chapter.
- Give each child a dress with flap pockets. Under each flap write a feeling that corresponds with Bill's emotions during this chapter, such as smugness, relief, anger.

> **How does Bill feel when the boys surround him at playtime?**
>
> **Can you explain Bill's feelings about Rapunzel as a heroine?**

## Day 5

- Read chapters 5 'The big fight' and 6 'Letting Paul win'. Ask the children why they think Bill could not let Paul win. How did Bill feel when he won the race? How did his feelings change when he saw the girls' faces? Reread the section in which the teacher organises the races. Discuss how this might affect the results.
- Look at a selection of boys and girls comics and discuss similarities and differences.
- Ask the children to draw a racetrack and to place Bill in a section of the race, such as at the beginning, in the middle and at the end. Draw a think bubble by each picture and Bill, and describe how he is feeling at each section.

## Day 6

- Read the final chapter 'Happy ending'. Discuss how Bill changes back into a boy again at the end of the story. Show the picture from page 89 on the interactive whiteboard. Ask the children if they think the experiences that Bill has had will change how he feels about and acts towards girls?
- Ask the children to write their own story with themselves as the main character who wakes up one day as a member of the opposite sex.
- Write a book review including their favourite character, favourite part of the story and how they would have liked the story to end.

# The Minpins

## Whole-class Starter

- Explain that this week the children are going to focus on a book by a famous author called Roald Dahl. Show the front cover of *The Minpins* and read the title. Ask for suggestions, from looking at the front cover, of what the book could be about. Explain that this is a longer book than they normally read and so it won't be possible to read it all in one go, but it will be an ongoing read that will last all week, with a different part being read each day.

### Day 1

- Read the beginning of the book (pages 5–12) finishing at the part where Billy cries out to his mum 'Save me!' Discuss why Billy disobeyed his mum? Billy thought his mum was making up the Forest of Sin. Why would she do that? Have the children ever done anything when their mum told them not to. Why? How do the children think Billy's mum feels when she realises he is missing?

## Focus of Learning
### To introduce younger children to a longer text

- Children draw or paint their own idea of what the characters in the Forest of Sin might look like.
- Look at the simile used to describe the Spittler – 'it was like the noise of a locomotive pulling out from a station'. Ask the children to draw their own Spittler and surround him with similes to describe how he looks, smells, moves and sounds.

### Day 2

- Read on to page 21 where Billy says that the Minpins' rooms are better than theirs at home. Discuss the description of the Minpin that Billy talks to. Put a picture of the Minpin on the interactive whiteboard and surround him with all the phrases that describe him, such as *ancient*, *minature face*, *severe expression*, *deeply wrinkled, eyes as bright as two stars.* Put a picture of a different Minpin on the board. Give each child a green paper leaf and ask them to write a phrase to describe the Minpin, such as *cheeky smile, rosy cheeks, as small as a pin.* Ask the children to place the phrases on the board around the Minpin. Read and discuss with the children.

- Give the children an A3 piece of paper and ask them to draw the tree from the story. Also give them some small pieces of paper to add to their tree to make flaps in which they can draw rooms and houses among the leaves.

- Make a Minpin miniature doll using matchsticks wool and beads. Write a description of their doll.

- Make a whole-class Minpin tree-house. Give each child a matchbox and ask them to turn it into a Minpin room.

## Day 3

- Read on to page 32 where Billy rides on the swan's back. Reread the part which says, 'Billy heard him talking to the robin in a kind of curious twitter. He couldn't understand a word of it. The robin nodded its head and flew off.' Put this picture on the interactive whiteboard with some empty speech bubbles and ask the children to make suggestions about what the Minpin and the robin were saying. Show some more pictures from the book in which the Minpins are riding on the birds or talking to the birds and add speech bubbles.

- Reread the description of the red hot, smoke-belching Gruncher. Ask the children to draw what they think the Gruncher looks like according to the description.

- Carry out some observational drawings of the birds from the story and watercolour.

- Ask the children to write what they think happens next in the story when Billy rides on the swan. For example, does he successfully destroy the Gruncher? Does the Gruncher eat the swan and kidnap Billy? Does Billy fly home and tell his mum?

## Day 4

- Read on to page 40 where Billy is taken back home by the swan. Look at the pictures of the part of the story that has just been read. Ask the children to add some thought bubbles.

- Mix different shades of red on flame-shaped pieces of paper using paint and pastels.

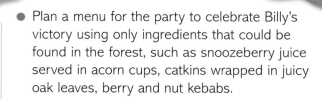

- Plan a menu for the party to celebrate Billy's victory using only ingredients that could be found in the forest, such as snoozeberry juice served in acorn cups, catkins wrapped in juicy oak leaves, berry and nut kebabs.

## Day 5

- Read to the end of the story. Take the children to a wooded area if you have one in your school, or if not, to a big tree. Reread the very end of the story where it says that Billy has kept the secret of the Minpins and hints that if you look closely, you might see them one day especially if you believe in magic. Ask the children to imagine what it would be like to meet the Minpins themselves. Where might they meet them? What might happen? What adventures might they have with the Minpins? Ask the children to write their own story in which they meet the Minpins.

- Draw a map of the events in the story.

- Ask the children to draw their own front cover for their story to illustrate the theme of the book and write a blurb for the back cover.

# The Twits

## Whole-class Starter

- Explain that throughout the week the class are going to focus on a book that has chapters within it. The book is *The Twits* by Roald Dahl (Puffin Books). Show the front cover and then the contents page, revealing the different chapters within the book.

Explain that an author uses chapters as a way of dividing a book into sections and in doing so makes the book easier to read and more interesting, particularly when a chapter ends on a cliffhanger, leaving the reader wanting more.

## Day 1

- Read chapters 1 to 4. Discuss what the children have learned so far in the story about

## Focus of Learning
To begin to understand how authors use chapters in books

Mr and Mrs Twit. Ask the children to work in pairs and give each pair two sticky notes. Ask the children to write on one sticky note what they know about Mr Twit and on the other what they know about Mrs Twit from reading the story so far. Discuss their responses.

- Reread the extracts describing Mr and Mrs Twit and ask the children to draw a picture of what they think Mr and Mrs Twit might look like.
- Give the children a picture of another character, drawn by the illustrator Quentin Blake, that they don't already know and ask them to write a description of that character.

## Day 2

- Read the chapters 'The glass eye' and 'Frog and wormy spaghetti'. Discuss why Mr and Mrs Twit enjoy playing tricks on each other. Ask the children if someone has ever played a trick on them or if they have ever played a trick. How do tricks make them feel? Can they think of other stories in which characters play tricks? For example, *Horrid Henry* by Francesca Simon (Orion Children's Books).

● Invent a new trick that Mr or Mrs Twit could play on each other and ask children to write and illustrate a new chapter for the book.

● Give children a selection of illustrations from these two chapters and ask them to add thought and speech bubbles.

## Day 3

● Read the chapters 'The funny walking stick', 'Mrs Twit has the shrinks' and 'Mrs Twit gets a stretching'. Discuss why this particular trick works so well. How does Mr Twit make it believable? Read the chapter 'Mrs Twit goes ballooning up'. Stop at the cliffhanger at the end of the chapter where Mrs Twit has floated off into the sky. Ask the children what they think will happen to Mr and Mrs Twit next?

● Ask the girls in the class to plan what they think happens to Mrs Twit. For example, how she might get down, where she might land, places she might visit. Would she miss Mr Twit or not? Would she send him a letter or email or postcard and what might it say? Ask the girls to write one of these from Mrs Twit to Mr Twit.

● Ask the boys in the class to plan what they think will happen to Mr Twit once Mrs Twit has gone. Will he miss her or not? Will he meet a new lady to marry? Will he turn into a nice character? Ask the boys to plan either a lonely hearts advert to find a new wife or a wanted poster to find Mrs Twit.

● At the end of the session read the chapters 'Mrs Twit comes ballooning down' and 'Mr Twit gets a horrid shock' to reveal what really happens.

## Day 4

● Read the chapters 'Hug tight sticky glue', 'Four sticky little boys', 'The great upside down

monkey circus', 'The roly poly bird to the rescue', 'No pie for Mr Twit', 'Still no pie for Mr Twit' and 'Mr and Mrs Twit go off to buy guns'. Reread the rhymes that the roly poly bird sings to the other birds. Practise singing together and add actions. Discuss the fact that the roly poly bird always sings his warnings in rhyme. Can the children work together to write a rhyme to warn children of the dangers or breaking rules in school.

● Play 'Hanging Monkey's Game'. Make a tree with hooks on the branches. Give each child five laminated monkeys with curly tails. Make a set of questions related to the story *The Twits* so far. Take it in turns to ask each child a question. If they answer correctly, they may hang a monkey on the tree. The winner is the first person to get rid of all their monkeys.

● Make a monkey mobile based on the ilustrations of the monkeys in the story.

● Draw, paint and collage a picture of the roly poly bird.

## Day 5

● Read the chapters 'Muggle Wump has an idea' and 'Mr and Mrs Twit are turned upside down'.

● Ask the children to draw a picture of another room in Mr and Mrs Twit's house that had been turned upside down, such as the kitchen, the garage.

● Make an upside down room in a shoebox.

● Finally, read and discuss the book to the end. Discuss the book as a whole. Put on the interactive whiteboard a list of the different chapters. Show how to rate them in terms of interest or excitement, such as give each chapter one, two or three stars for interest or excitement and give the climax of the story five stars. Discuss how chapters have different purposes, such as to introduce characters, to build tension, suspense and action. Produce a graph on the board charting the ratings of each chapter.

# War Game

## Whole-class Starter

- Before reading *War Game* by Michael Foreman (Puffin Books), discuss with the children when and where the story is set. Explain that they are going to explore what this story tells us about wartime and how war affects people.

### Day 1

- Read chapter 1 'The kick off' and discuss what the children have learned about the four characters so far. Refer back to the title page, which shows Michael Foreman has written the story in memory of his uncles, and discuss that this is a fictional story but with real characters. Reread the conversation between the boys about the war. Discuss what the boys think about war. Also look

## Focus of Learning

**To empathise with characters and debate moral dilemmas shown in text**

at the enlisting posters in the book. How do they persuade the boys to go to the recruiting office? Go into role with the teaching assistant – one as a sergeant major and one as a devoted mother. Present the arguments 'for' and 'against' going to war.

- Ask the children to write a list of reasons for and against going to war.
- Ask the children to design their own enlisting poster.
- Ask the children to write a diary entry from the point of few of one of the characters discussing what has happened on that day.

### Day 2

- Begin to read chapter 2 'The adventure'. At the end of page 17 stop and reread the final sentence – 'they had a lot of explaining to do when they got home that evening'. Ask the children what the author means by that. Discuss who might be at home and what their reactions might be. Read to the end of the chapter. Why were the lads 'disappointed' at basic training? Why does it say on page 22 'the adventure had really started'? Why did Will feel 'strangely alone' on the ship?

- Draw and label a Tommie's uniform and discuss the reasons for the different parts.
- Draw a map of Europe identifying the countries that were at war during the First World War.

## Day 3

- Read the next chapter 'To the Front'. Discuss how the story changes and compare the contrast in mood and pictures from page 31 onwards. Ask the children to list how things have changed for the boys and to think about how the boys might feel now. Look at the picture of the trenches. Discuss what life was like for the men living at the trenches. Make an interactive whiteboard presentation of pictures, accounts and film clips that give a further insight into life in the trenches.
- Ask the children to write a letter home to their family as one of the boys in the story. Write on tea-bagged paper.
- Give children a selection of pictures of men in the trenches and ask them to add speech and thought bubbles to the pictures.
- Look at Michael Foreman's artwork in the book. Ask the children to reproduce one of his pictures using watercolour pencils.

## Day 4

- Read chapter 4 'No Man's Land' up to page 77. Discuss the difference between life in No Man's Land before Christmas Eve and life in No Man's Land at Christmas. Use a selection of illustrations from the story and scan them into an interactive whiteboard. Look at each picture and ask the children to work with a partner to discuss the different things that the soldiers in the pictures might be thinking according to the story.
- Give the children a selection of quotes from

the text to discuss as a group. For example, 'The clock of death had stopped ticking', 'The bodies were mixed up together ... a joint burial was held on the halfway line'. What is the author telling us?

- Look at the page with Christmas gifts and messages from the king and queen. Design a Christmas parcel, draw and write the gifts inside and add a note from the king.
- Write a Christmas letter to one of the boys from their parents at home. Include their parents' feelings and news from home.

## Day 5

- Read chapter 4 'No Man's Land' from page 77 to the end. What does the author say happened on Boxing Day? Why do they send a note telling 'the Tommies to please keep their heads down'? When fresh troops from Prussia are sent in, how does that change things? As the English troops attack, the author uses a lot of language associated with football such as 'Will in a centre-forward position', 'Billy on the wing', 'they were all tackled at once'. Why does the author use this language? What happens to the lads? Why does Will share his water with the enemy? After finishing the book, reflect with the children on the title *War Game*. Why did the author choose this title?

- Draw a pictorial story map using pictures and arrows and a summary of each part of the story. Identify the introduction, build up, climax, and resolution of the story.
- Look at the final page and discuss what the poppies symbolise and why the author has used them in the book. Create a selection of artwork related to poppies. The children could sketch poppies, use chalk pastels to create a field of poppies, use a ripped paper effect to create a poppy collage, make a clay poppy tile or print poppies.

# Winnie the Pooh

## Whole-class Starter

- Explain that the children are going to be reading the stories of *Winnie the Pooh* by A.A. Milne (Egmont Books, Methuen).

### Day 1

- Read the story 'In Which We are Introduced to Winnie-the-Pooh and Some Bees'. Discuss what the children know at the end of the story and what they have learned about Pooh Bear. For example, his name is Mr Saunders, he likes honey and is a bit greedy, and he is a silly bear. Put large pictures of the other characters in the Winnie the Pooh stories on the interactive whiteboard. What do the children know about these characters and what can they guess from the pictures? Explain that throughout the week they will add to these as they find out more about each character.
- Draw pictures of each of the characters and annotate with words related to each one.
- Paint and collage giant characters.

## Focus of Learning
**To recognise automatically an increasing number of high-frequency words**

### Day 2

- Read the Disney story '*Winnie the Pooh and Tigger too*' (Disney, Random House). Ask the children if they can remember how Tigger says his name; for example, he sounds it out T–i–double g–er. Show Tigger's name broken down phonetically on the interactive whiteboard. Explain that Tigger is using his letter sounds to help spell his name and that we can use these most of the time to help us read. Prepare a presentation on the interactive whiteboard of Tigger bouncing onto the screen. On each Tigger should be a grapheme that when put together will spell a word. Ask the children to blend the phonemes to read the word, such as ch–i–p–s, f–l–a–g, m–oo–n.

- Play 'Bouncing Bonanza'. Prepare word cards that include phonetically regular words. Make a set of corresponding picture cards and place them around a large hall or space. Split the children into two teams and give each team a spacehopper so they can bounce like Tigger! Choose a child from each team and give the pair a word to read. The first person to bounce to the corresponding picture wins a point for their team.
- Play 'Tap the Tigger'. Prepare an interactive whiteboard presentation with three Tiggers bouncing onto the screen each with a phonetically regular word. Only one of these should be the correct spelling. The children take it in turns to hold a 'splatter' and try to splat the correct word as you read it out.

## Day 3

- Read the story 'Eeyore loses a tail'. Discuss the character of Owl – it says in the story he is wise. Is this true? Put the picture of Owl's house on the interactive whiteboard. What can the children tell you? Discuss that it is difficult to read the notices outside his house because of the spellings. Discuss how not all words can be read or spelt by using letter sounds as some words are tricky words and just need to be learned. Explain that they are going to practise reading these tricky words. On the interactive whiteboard, show a picture of Pooh Bear's honey pot. Explain that bumblebees have a sting in their tail just like these tricky words and show bumblebees that buzz onto the screen with a high-frequency word that is phonetically irregular, such as *said*, *was*, *saw*. Help the children to read these words and discuss the tricky bits in each word.
- Paint large bumblebees that can then be added to a classroom spelling display with high-frequency words on them.
- Give the children simple sentences in which they identify words with the 'sting in their tail', that is, phonetically irregular words. Draw a bumblebee around the tricky part of the word.

- Play 'Read with Speed'. Make a set of high-frequency words on giant bumble bee cards. Split the children into two groups. Each group takes it in turn to read the words one at time on the bumblebees. The object is to see who can get the furthest and which team can read them the quickest.

## Day 4

- Discuss the setting of the Winnie the Pooh stories. Show the picture of Hundred Acre Wood inside the front cover of both the original Winnie the Pooh stories and the Disney versions and discuss the similarities and differences. Discuss other things that the children could add, such as steps up to Tigger's House, Rabbit's carrot patch.
- As a class project, create a Hundred Acre Wood using collage material. Label the appropriate features on the Hundred Acre Wood map using phonetic spellings such as in the style of the book.
- Draw and collage characters onto your own Hundred Acre Wood map.
- Play 'Hunt through the Hundred Acre Wood'. Make a board game of the Hundred Acre Wood. On the board place bees with words on them. The object is to move through the wood landing on as many bees with words as possible. If the children can read the word on the bee, they collect one of the characters. The object is to collect all the characters.

# Stand-out Display — Haiku

His wishes came true,
He felt mightier than all,
He wished to change back.

His wishes were heard,
"A man once more you shall be!"
The man was content.

'Haiku' is a form of Japanese poetry.

We read a Japanese folk tale called 'The Stonecutter' and wrote our own Haiku poems.

A stonecutter, then
A rich man, the sun, a cloud,
A rock, then a man.

Haiku poems rarely rhyme.

He saw a rich man,
All his wishes were granted,
He ended a man.

The stonecutter wished,
To be rich and powerful,
He was unhappy.

Haiku poems always have 3 lines.

The first and last lines of a Haiku have 5 syllables and the middle line has 7 syllables.

## About Haiku

- Haiku is a form of Japanese Poetry which consists of three lines per poem. The first line always has five syllables, the second seven, and the third five. The main lesson on Haiku poetry will creatively encourage students to learn about the poetry and culture of Japan, and will also help in their understanding of what a syllable is and how they form words and sentences.

- See page 36 for more!

## Focus of Learning
To develop an understanding of poetry from other cultures
To identify syllables within words